God's Master Plan

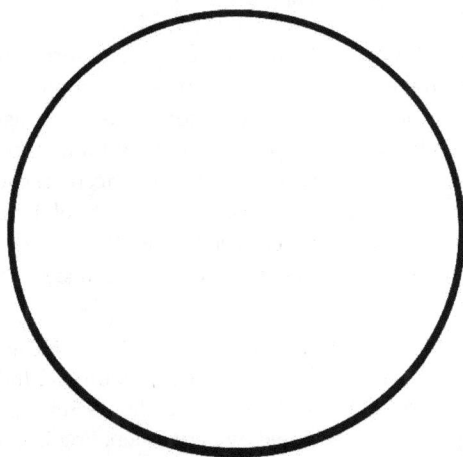

A book by

RHETT OTIS

Missage Media

God's Master Plan
by RHETT OTIS

Summary: Findings from a holistic investigation of God's master plan for humanity and how God is dealing with the current conflict with Satan in the heavens, why some names are blotted from the Book of Life, how our heart, soul and spirit interact and where they go after death, what Hades and Heaven is and why Paradise is now empty, the superbody refabrications, the Eternal Fire, what to expect in the end time events and the future mass extinctions, angelic transportation devices (ATDs), and the seventh Era yet to come. Discusses God's precepts for having an abundant life in Christ, successful relationships, marriage, and raising children.

ISBN: 978-0-9829547-9-9
Library of Congress Control Number: 2020904172
Copyright: 1-8592186131
Text copyright © 2023 by Rhett Otis

Cover and Book Art by Rhett Otis © 2023. Webb's First Deep Field and Earth from NASA and STScI. Missage Media - Charlottesville, Virginia

Thanks to my patient wife,
who has made my life so enjoyable

1

The Investigation

You may, like me, desire to know more of God's master plan for us, and why this conflict in the Universe is now causing so much chaos here on Earth. Would you like to have more clarity on what your life here on Earth is really about, why God wants loving relationships with each one of us, and how God uses our trials to draw us closer to Him?

Would you like to be more grounded in solid biblical principles to strengthen personal relationships, to know more of God's precepts for growing enjoyable marriages, and principles for raising kids who are pleasant to be with and desire to serve the Lord? Understanding how our spirit, heart and soul interacts helps us understand and manage our deep internal motives, and knowing how God designed them to work together helps us to better know ourselves, relate better with others, and make wise decisions.

Have you wondered where human souls go after we die, and how this changed after Jesus died on the cross? Why it's so important to not have our name blotted out from God's Book of Life? What Paradise, Heaven and Hades is, what Heaven will be like, and what we will be doing there for all of eternity? Why Satan is now the god of Earth and the source of our planet's problems? Why our omnipotent and supremely powerful God hasn't already put an end to Satan and to evil? Why it seems inevitable that bad events are about to occur? My investigation into these matters has increased my faith and relationship with God, and I hope this summary of my investigation into these things will encourage you also.

Heart, Soul, and Spirit Preview

The thoughts of our soul and the intentions of our spirit are closely entwined within the decisions of our heart, but God's living and powerful Word can discern this difference between our thoughts and our intentions. Although they are very closely connected, our soul, heart and spirit are distinctly different! (Hebrews 4:12)

The Hebrew "nephesh" is used for both animal and human **souls**, or **life**. The Bible doesn't say the souls of animals survive death as human souls do, but knowing they have souls helps explain why animals have emotions, such as intelligent dolphins with their enhanced self-control and social skills. Our valiant Australian Shepard feels brave and fears the unknown, is often elated to see us, and enjoys companionship. God gave animals these feelings; He gave them life, or souls, as He did to humans. There is much said lately about the human soul, yet scripture places more emphasis on our heart and spirit! (Genesis 1:20,24,30; 2:7,19; 9:4)

Our "**heart**" is our will and what we use to make our decisions and believe in God. We need to diligently guard our heart because it determines what we do in our life. (Proverbs 4:23: Mark 15:19; Romans 10:10)

Our **spirit** provides our intents and influences and urges us to do things at times. We should consider our spirit's intents and our soul's thoughts and desires, but our heart ultimately decides what we will do. Proverbs 16:32 says we need to control our spirit. God's Holy Spirit enters and dwells in us after we believe in God, and provides us with God's intentions. We decide in our heart what to do with these gentle whispers and intents from the Holy Spirit. We don't have to obey God, and if we do disobey, we can quench this influence of the Holy Spirit. The Holy Spirit also connects all believers as One Spirit! In realizing this, it dawned on me why I sometimes think of someone and pray for them, and later find out they really needed prayers at that time! It's not some physic ability, it is the Holy Spirit connecting us and softly whispering to us when others need our prayers! Isn't that so cool? It's amazing. (1 Thessalonians 5:19)

The Lord also has a heart and a soul (Jeremiah 32:41), but angels and heavenly beings from God's heavenly realm are just said to have spirits (1 Kings 22:21; Ezekiel 10:17; Hebrews 1:14), so we have more in common with the Lord than with angels (Genesis 1:26-27).

The old expression "follow your heart" implies that we should pursue our soul's desires and our spirit's deeply-felt aspirations. Since the human heart, biblically, is our will, we should first *guard* our heart because we use it to make our decisions, then *consider* our spirit's intents and our soul's thoughts and desires, and *then* decide in our heart what to do. As Proverbs 16:32 points out, we should control our spirit, not follow it. People who allow their spirit to control them aren't thinking things through deeply enough. When our heart relinquishes decision-making control to our spirit it makes us vulnerable to hasty and poorly thought-out decisions. (Proverbs 4:23, 23:19-21; Malachi 2:13-16)

Thinking, Fast and Slow, by Daniel Kahneman, explains how we tend to instinctively think fast, and as a consequence we intuitively come to a wrong conclusion. Daniel points out we need to think carefully and deliberately and engage our intellect so we can make better decisions. This slow, deep thinking engages our heart to consult with our spirit's intents and our soul's thoughts and feelings before we carefully make a wiser decision. For a believer, "slow thinking" includes mediation, reading God's Word and prayer. In other words, we should allow time for concentrated thought and prayer before making important decisions.

Knowing how our soul, spirit and heart work together helps us become more aware of the differences between our desires, intents, thoughts, feelings, motives and desires. The "OUR HEART", "SOUL", "SPIRIT", and "The Abundant Life" sections are almost entirely composed of woven together scripture, and for me they radiate with the Holy Spirit and God's love. I hope you will find this to be true also, and that the truth in these will motivate and inspire you every day—

We should be glad when our trials come, because it is through patiently enduring them that we grow in our faith and our character grows stronger. The burden Jesus places on us is light and easy. Our **soul** finds rest when we make our requests known to Him, learn to trust Him by carefully reading God's word, and walk in harmony with Him. He is the Father of our **spirit** and we are His children, and this is why He wants to help us with our painful problems; to unburden us, heal us and give us peace. The Lord comes close to those who have a humble and broken and contrite **heart**. He sends His Spirit into our hearts, and we cry, "Daddy, Father!" God's Spirit dwells in our new adopted heart to comfort, teach and bless us.

The Clouds of Heaven and White Spaceships

Was Revelation written with the ancient Greek words that best fit our *current* time perspective? Consider that Revelation 19:11-14 says when Jesus and His army returns to Earth they will be sitting upon or residing within white "hippos". The Greek "hippos" means something barrel-shaped like a hippopotamus, and is usually translated as "horse". So, all we are *actually* told is that Jesus and His army will be within or upon some type of white, barrel-shaped transportation.

First, a great cloud conceals Jesus and His army as they descend towards Earth from space. The descent of this great cloud towards Earth takes some time, since the rebellious rulers of Earth can see the sign of Jesus coming in these great clouds in space, and the beast angel Abaddon has enough time to gather a massive army to fight Jesus. Then, Jesus descends from this great cloud, just as He was lifted into a cloud when he ascended from Earth long ago. (Acts 1:9-11)

When this great cloud reveals Jesus and His army, will they be returning on white horses, or be in white spaceships? Horses and chariots were the means of transportation thousands of years ago. But, if Revelation was translated with today's perspective in mind, "hippos" could be translated as "Angelic Transportation Devices" (ATDs). God created physics and angels. No doubt Jesus and His angels know more about quantum physics, and have fantastic transportation devices that are much more highly advanced than anything humanity has! However Jesus returns, it is going to be super cool!

Consider the movies about terrible space invaders who attack Earth. The vulnerable humans fight back and somehow defeat these space invaders. I enjoy watching science fiction movies, but find it interesting there is a common theme that these space invaders are evil. Jesus made Earth, and God owns it. Satan has just taken it over, at least in part; and we humans haven't been doing all that great of a job caring for it. Jesus *will* take it back and reign over Earth for a very peaceful and prosperous one-thousand years. No doubt, when Jesus returns in this great cloud, He will be regarded as an alien invader to those unbelieving humans who are still living on Earth. Maybe that is why I suspect Jesus and His army will return in white spacecrafts; it fits the profile of what humanity has been conditioned to fear and hate.

God's Orbiting City and iEarth 7 Preview

In Heaven, will we sit on clouds and play harps, or will we have upgraded superbodies and live *with* God on an amazingly renovated Planet Earth? An Earth so fantastic that *Avatar's* Pandora will seem pale in comparison? God gave us a few clues about this—

After the seventh trumpet has sounded near the end of the tribulation, in Revelation 16 the sea is ruined, the mountains are leveled and the islands have fled. If you are thinking of waiting this out on an island, consider that even if your boat withstands the massive tsunami waves from the planetary earthquake that levels all of the mountains and islands, the oceans will become so polluted that everything in it dies.

God then heals our planet and Jesus reigns over planet Earth for one-thousand peaceful years. The animals become so peaceful that lions will even eat grass! With peace on Earth and long-life spans, technology may exponentially advance so rapidly that the technology of science fiction movies will seem juvenile in comparison. At the end of this utopian one-thousand years, Satan, who was locked up at the beginning of it, is released and once again wreaks havoc and turns the nations against Jesus. They surround the holy city that Jesus is in with His believers. Fire comes down from God and burns up the attacking army, and likely the entire planet; we may be like Shadrach, Meshach and Abed-Nego in the fiery furnace! (2 Peter 3:7-10; Revelation 20:9)

In Revelation 21, after our Lord's millennial one-thousand-year reign ends with this fire, God says He will now make all things new for His new Earth. Since God's last six Eras were here on Earth (as I've come to realize), and assuming that He will renovate our planet once again (which it seems to indicate), what will God's awesome seventh Era be like, His new iEarth 7? It will no longer have vast oceans, so our planet's water may run through massive artery and vein-like aquafers to distribute geothermal heat and water the plants and trees as it may have done in prior Eras. I picture an interlacing of gentle hills, lakes, streams, waterfalls, Jurassic Era redwoods and giant sequoias, amazing new fantastic kinds of trees, plants and animals, and new relationships with those who dwell among the stars. We may even have the ability to teleport, as Jesus could. When we look up, will we see God's new translucent gold city orbiting overhead?

When God the Father dwells with us, will His fantastic new city also serve as an orbiting interstellar gateway space city for both humans and those who dwell in the heavens, as Revelation 21:10 seems to indicate?— John is taken to a very high altitude (many translations state this is as a "great high mountain", but this Greek "oros" simply indicates that John was lifted "exceedingly high above the plains". Also keep in mind that Earth's mountains have all been leveled *before* this occurs). John observes an angel measuring God's beautiful new city as it descends towards Earth. The angel is told to measure the city, the city's gates, and the wall. The city is square- 1,400 miles by 1,400 miles, the altitude is 1,400 miles, and the wall is 200 feet. Did you catch the measurement of the gates? They are 1,400 miles high!

1,400-mile-high gates would stick out from Earth's surface like an enormous appendage! However, if this city *orbits* Earth, then it makes a lot of sense why these gates will be at an altitude of 1,400-miles. The passage never states that God's city actually comes to rest on Earth. Also, the Greek "hupos" is used for this gate "height", which means "altitude in the sky"! People long ago would likely have difficulty understanding how a solid gold city could stay in Middle Earth Orbit. They didn't know of the Roche limits for planetary orbit. I think it is super cool that, *if* God's new city is to be 1,400 miles high in lower Middle Earth orbit with a jeweled 200-foot-thick dome in the less hazardous lower part of the Van Allen radiation belt, it does comply with our current laws of physics. It also states God will make all things new, so it doesn't necessarily *have* to comply with our current classic or relative laws of physics. The city's gates always stay open. How could this be? Movies like *Jupiter Descending* have no difficulty depicting how space gates can open. God Himself will dwell there, so if He wants the gates to always stay open, or have His city in geostationary orbit, or wants to make another Universe, He will do it.

What does the Bible say about these extraterrestrials, those who dwell among the stars, and what interest do they have in humanity? It does say a little— Ephesians 3 explains that from the very beginning God kept His mysterious eternal plan a secret from them. Part of God's purpose, of Jesus dying for our sins so that those who believe can receive eternal life, was to display His wisdom to the rulers and authorities of these unseen places in the Universe— God reconciled all things to Himself, the things in heaven and the things on Earth. (Colossians 1:20)

There *are* extraterrestrials. It's biblical. God will reconcile those who dwell in the heavens with humanity, and it could be that God's new city will orbit Earth as a space station. Jesus said, "In my Father's house are many mansions." When Satan is finally cast out of the heavens, those who "dwell in the heavens" will rejoice— are they now living in these celestial mansions? (John 14:2; Colossians 1:20; Revelation 6:13,9:1-19,12:12)

It may be difficult to visualize quantum-based fifth-dimension extraterrestrial angels without our being biased by their humanistic portrayal in movies. I can't recall any science fiction movie where an incredible omnipotent being with genuine goodwill and love for all creates the Universe, angels, cherubim and many other things, makes six Eras of living creatures and humans on Earth, and knows them all by name. A God who allows humans to have free will and disobey Him if they choose. A God who patiently works through problems and issues over millions of years, predestines events billions of years in advance, dwells outside of time, and is all knowing.

God's realm and angels have a certain association with light— God dwells in an unapproachable light. When the Lord spoke with Daniel, His face was like lightning and His eyes were like flaming torches. When Jesus became transfigured and spoke with Moses and Elijah, His face shone like the sun and his clothes were brilliantly lit with light. The angel who rolled back the stone from the tomb of Jesus had a face filled with a lightning-like light, and had clothes as white as snow. Moses' face glowed with so much light after being in the Lord's presence that he frightened others. This indicates our future upgraded bodies will also be filled with some quantum-enabled light, a fifth-dimension energy not as we now dimly understand it in quantum physics, but an eternal spiritual lifeforce energy radiating with a kind of light that is difficult for us to physically see, or understand, from our current perspective. Jesus teleported through walls and rose into the air after His resurrection. When He appears, we will be like Him, because we will see Him as He really is, so we may also share some of these same attributes.

Facts are stubborn things;
and whatever may be our wishes, our inclinations,
or the dictates of our passion, they cannot alter
the state of facts and evidence
– John Adams

End Times Preview – Great Signs and Wonders

The Bible tells of a constitution with specific written requirements that governs all beings in the Universe, both angels and human. Long ago the humans of Planet Earth were condemned by these written requirements. God the Father, who dwells in Eternity, is called the Lord of Hosts in the Old Testament, and His Son is known as the Angel of the Lord (Zechariah 1:12). This Angel of the Lord was born as Jesus in human form to fulfil these written requirements by dying on the cross to reconcile and bring together His Heavenly family with His Earthly family. Jesus provided a way for those humans who believe in Him and want to be on His side to later be enabled to live forever physically. Powerful, and currently unseen, angels and extraterrestrial powers can now no longer condemn humanity because Jesus disarmed them, making a universal or galactic public spectacle of them, and triumphing over them. In the future Jesus will bring universal peace, and every resident on Earth, and every resident on other planets, all of those in the Universe, will bow to Jesus. Jesus will finally reconcile His family in heaven and His family on Earth. God's golden city will descend towards Earth and, as it seems to say, orbit Earth to serve as the Lord's gateway space station for both humans and angels. Believers will then judge angels.

At the end of a great past or future war in heaven (determining if this is a past or future event is complex, considering that time itself varies, such as the time dilation of near lightspeed space travel), Michael and the angels on the Lord's side physically cast Satan and his angels out of heaven and down to Earth. Those who are dwelling in the Universe rejoice when Satan and his angels are cast to Earth, and a mighty voice says, "Woe to you of Earth, for what is about to come!"

Revelation 6 unseals an overview of how six events will impact humanity. Revelation 8 and 9 are written from a Universal perspective and announce with trumpets six end-time events with celestial origins. These events occur after our nations become perplexed by the behavior of our sun, moon and the raging waves of Earth's oceans. (Luke 21:25-26)

Some of the celestial events in Revelation 8 and 9 seem to involve at least two massive angelic transportation devices (ATDs):

1) An enormous storm of small meteorites flame through the atmosphere and cause massive fires on one third of Earth's land area.

2) A great mass like a very large mountain falls to Earth and destroys one third of the sea creatures and ships.

3) The massive radioactive starship Wormwood comes burning down through the atmosphere like a torch. The debris falling to Earth contaminates one third of Earth's fresh water. Many die from radioactive poisoning.

4) A massive object begins orbiting Earth that is so enormous it blocks out one third of the sky (the sun, moon and stars). This seems to describe a mammoth spaceship that is orbiting Earth.

5) The Abyss portal is opened with a key amidst dense smoke, and a vast winged army of abominable stinging creatures emerge, which could be physical incarnations of the demons that Jesus had commanded into this abyss (Luke 10:17-20). Abaddon, a highly-intelligent and destructive angel, also emerges. He controls these creatures that cause tremendous pain, but not death, for five months.

6) Four angels are unbound and they lead a vast army of 200 million riders who invade Earth (possibly coming from the mammoth ATD orbiting Earth). These riders have armor with superhero-like colors of fiery red, hyacinth blue and sulfur yellow. They are in or upon barrel-shaped transportation devices with fiery fronts which emit highly toxic sulfur dioxide gas and brimstone. Located in the back of these flying devices is some malicious, cunning, and deadly technology.

Later, Revelation 17:8 explains that the "beast" who ascends out of the Abyss "was, and is not, and yet is". This must be Abaddon, since he is the destructive angel who ascends from the Abyss— The stories of Greek Mythology about their god's improprieties and affairs with human women, such as Apollon, may have originated from the angels who had offspring with human women in the time of Noah. Genesis 6 says these giant offspring were "men of renown", so well before the time of the Greeks there were well-known stories circulating about their exploits. The angels of Noah's time, these wandering stars, left their heavenly habitation and sinned, unlike the angels in heaven. God sent these sinful celestial angels to Tartarus, the deepest abyss of Hades. Abaddon was present long ago, but is not now because he is in the bottomless Abyss, and yet will come back physically to Earth's surface.

Humanity marvels at the great military and oration abilities of Abaddon, and then worships him after Abaddon miraculously heals from a deadly head injury. If Abaddon's humanlike "bio-shell" is an extension of his spirit, then it is logical that he could rebuild it since his life force is not dependent on his "bio-shell", as human souls are. Soon afterwards, his false prophet has humanity build a sentient "image" to help track down and kill any who will not worship Abaddon. If one were to write long ago of a highly-advanced artificial intelligence that infiltrates Earth's electronic devices to track down any who won't worship Abaddon, the account would read very similar to what is written in Revelation 13:14-15. A conscious intelligence like that of *The Terminator* or the *Age of Ultron* movies, but it is at the command of an extremely intelligent, and very well-spoken, articulate, highly-advanced extraterrestrial life form, Abaddon, who can't be biologically destroyed, and whose false prophet likely uses a computerized sentient life to target believers for efficient termination. "Abaddon" literally means destroyer.

Assuming angels are technologically illiterate white-robed beings with large wings using 5,000-year-old human chariot technology might be part of the great lie to come. Will wayward angels deceive humanity by posing as evolutionarily-advanced extraterrestrials using **technological great signs and wonders**? (Matthew 24:24; 2 Thessalonians 2:9-11)

Jesus was made a little lower than the angels when He came to Earth to reconcile the things on this rebellious Earth with the "other things" in the Universe, so it stands to reason that these "other things" have highly-advanced technologies. Angels are much more advanced and greater in power and might than humans! Some angels are with God the Father who dwells in eternity, and some angels, evidently a vast assortment of them, dwell elsewhere in the Universe and very likely have been around much longer than humanity has, and with a vastly superior knowledge of exotic technologies that we know nothing about, which will likely be perceived by humanity as "alien tech". Humanity knows virtually nothing of quantum physics, gravitational waves, or dark energy. At one time humanity thought reproduction and healing were miracles, but now that we know more of it, we just think it is amazing. We know so little of the Universe, and nothing of its many types of inhabitants, but some day we will know much more of angelic exopsychology, physiology and physics than we do now. (John 5:4; 1 Corinthians 13:9-12)

Humanity has determined so far that everything God has made follows very precise scientific physical formulas and biological principles.

What if we tried to imagine Earth, and the only evidence we had were descriptions of two people walking on the sand, a sports car, and a mongoose. Could we then possibly imagine what Earth is like in all of its complexity of life, ecosystems, and the last several thousand years of modern human history? And so, we can't possibly know about the many other spirit-enabled sentient extraterrestrial life forms that God has created with all of their complexity and history and highly advanced technologies that may even go back for billions of years!

Did you know that Revelation 18 explained long ago that humanity will use a planetary merchandising system of cargo ships to transport vast quantities of costly and extravagant merchandise between countries? This ancient account lists what was costly merchandise at the time it was written a few thousand years ago— fine linen, purple, silk, ivory, food, **four-wheeled carriages**, and all manner of precious things that our souls lust for and desire (the Greek "rheda" is usually translated as chariots, but in ancient Rome a **rheda** was actually a **four-wheeled traveling carriage**, which was the closest thing there was to an **automobile** at the time it was written). This prophesy of Revelation 18 accurately depicts our current global economy with its costly merchandise shipments of designer clothes, food, extravagant smart phones, and the automobiles that our souls desire and lust for.

Revelation 18:23 also reveals that our vast global system will deceive the nations with her "pharmakeia". "Pharmakeia" is usually translated as "sorceries", but **pharmakeia** is the Greek root word for pharmacy, and implies that this deception involves both legal and illegal **drugs and medicines**. God made medicines for humanity to use, but, like most things, something God made for good can be twisted into evil. Drugs are now a global epidemic— Narcotic-based prescription drugs, although legal, are highly addictive with widespread abuse, as well as mood-altering drugs and recreational drugs. Could it be said that the nations are now deceived by illegal drugs, and by some legalized drugs? Revelation 18:23 accurately depicts our global dependency on drugs!

End time events are scary, but it is just a temporary transition for believers. After we die, our soul and spirit leave our physical body and goes on to live with the Lord. God promised to someday give us new and vastly upgraded physical bodies. We may look back in pity on how inferior our old biological bodies were. The end game is not to do whatever it takes to stay alive in the tribulation, but to help others, and to reach others for Christ so they too can live on eternally!

Revelation 13:7, 17:6 and 20:4 makes it clear that many believers are to be slaughtered. The few who do survive to the end will be saved when their bodies are physically transformed into new ones as they still live! Imagine playing a computer game which gifts you just one life-force to help others. Whenever your life-force ends then you are guaranteed to level up for a vastly improved eternal body with amazing abilities in a much better place. This eternal guarantee of physically and spiritually leveling up after we die is what believers refer to as our "Hope".

Our Hope is our guarantee of our future life with Christ, not in stockpiling food and living in a hole in the ground to wait it out until Jesus returns. Expect to die, but try to die well. Jesus spoke of one who buried their talent in a hole and did nothing to invest it. Our treasure is our faith in Jesus, and our Hope is our future life with Christ and God. Investing our treasure and using our talent is being a witness for Jesus, so we shouldn't hide our talents! Yet, Revelation 13:10 warns us to be prudent, to not go into captivity or lead others into captivity, and if we fight with guns we will die with guns. Don't go into captivity and don't fight. This is God's advice— try and survive so we can help others.

Understanding the magnitude of God's predicament with Satan helps us understand our current state of eminent death, pain, sickness, wars and evil acts. The next chapter discusses what God has told us of this vast Universal conflict and how He is going to handle it. Humanity plays an important role in God's predestined plan of dealing with Satan's discord in the heavens, and we are now caught in the midst of this predestined heavenly war! So, if you feel like things are chaotic, well, they are! God, in His perfect time, will soon finish dealing with this Universal dissonance. We just need to be patient.

References used in composing this first chapter— Genesis 6:1-5, 18:1-19:22; 28:12-13; Exodus 34:29-30; Enoch 6; 2 Kings 2:12, 6:17; Isaiah 57:15; Daniel 7:13-14, 9:21, 10:6-19; Zechariah 5:1-6:7; Matthew 17:2, 22:30, 24:30, 26:64, 28:2; Mark 9:2, 13:26, 14:62; Luke 2:14, 21:25-27, 24:36; John 1:51, 3:16-17, 5:4, 20:26; Acts 1:9, 5:19, 8:39-40, 12:7 23:6, 24:15; Romans 8:20-24,38; I Corinthians 4:9, 6:3, 11:10; 15:38-53; Galatians 1:8; Ephesians 1:10, 20-23, 2:6, 3:10-14, 4:10, 6:12; Philippians 2:10; Colossians 1:15-20, 2:14-15; 1 Thessalonians 4:13-18; 1 Timothy 6:15-16; Hebrews 1:4, 2:5-9, 13:2,21; 1 Peter 3:19; 2 Peter 2:4-11; 1 John 3:2-3; Jude 6-15; Revelation 1:7, chapters 8 and 9, 12:12, 13:3-18, 17:8,18, 19:19, 21:2.

The Investigation

Litigation and investigating medical fraud have long been a part of my career. It occurred to me, while writing *God and Humans*, that I was instinctively using investigative techniques by using a Hebrew and Greek Interlinear Dictionary and doing reverse searches with the Strong's Concordance. Studying the source evidence of how words are used throughout the Old and New Testaments helps determine the truth and context in the original biblical text, and what these passages are actually indicating. If my viewpoint, or yours, isn't supported by the infallible Word of God, then it may not be true, regardless of how many others think it to be true, and therefore only what is strongly supported by scripture ought to be embraced as strongly-held beliefs.

After growing up in a very conservative Christian group in California, I gradually came to realize that some of what I had believed to be true in the depth of my soul was actually in error. Like peeling back the layers of an onion, I gradually came to realize how wrong I had been about some things that I had believed to be true to the core of my heart. Even my own conscience was flawed— some things that I had thought were wrong were actually acceptable, and some things that I had thought were right were actually quite wrong. This deeply disturbing, and painful, experience helped me realize how many of us have strongly-felt beliefs that we haven't prayerfully studied and could be wrong about. We tend to assume that we already know the answers and must defend what we think, and we tend to discount any new information that conflicts with our opinions. Like most humans, Christians tend to unquestioningly believe what their respected friends believe, especially if they heard or read about it when they were young. So, in conducting my investigation, little consideration was given to the opinions of others. But, I *was* relieved to find that others had arrived at some of the same conclusions! (See the suggested reading at the end of this book.)

If something conflicts with your beliefs, I hope you will read the references and meditate and pray. We can be deceived and not even realize it. The Holy Spirit gently urges us towards the truth. (John 14:26)

With regard to matters requiring thought:
the less people know and understand about them, the more positively
they attempt to argue concerning them – Galileo Galilei

Discovers Conflict with Views or Beliefs

Re-evaluates and Examines Bible Again

Reads Bible and Develops Views and Beliefs

Walks in Peace with God

Believer Values Truth

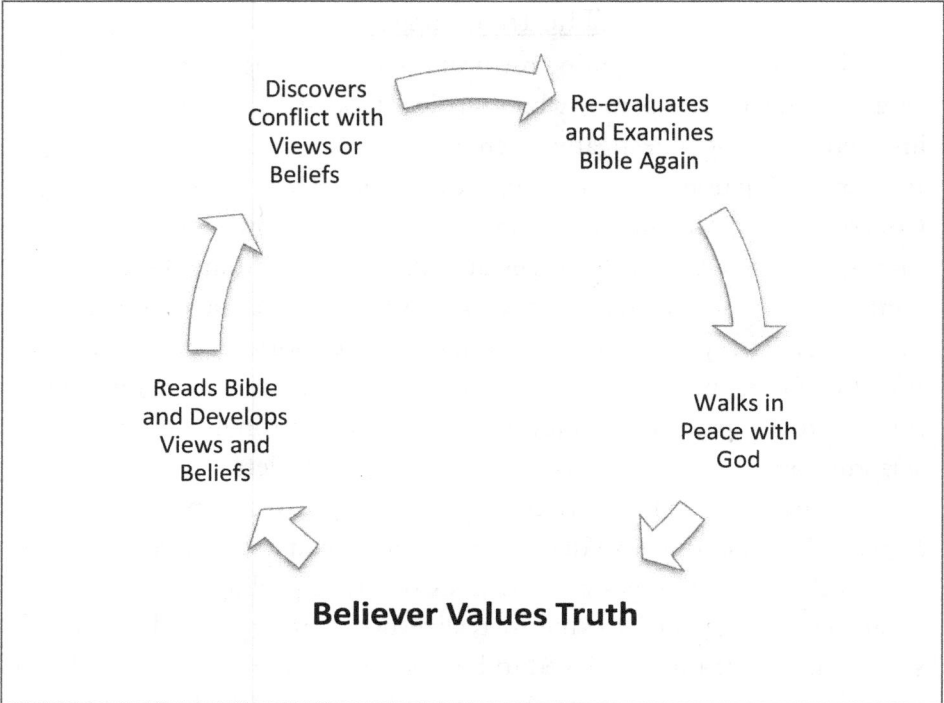

Test everything that is said. Hold on to what is good - 1 Thessalonians 5:19 NLT

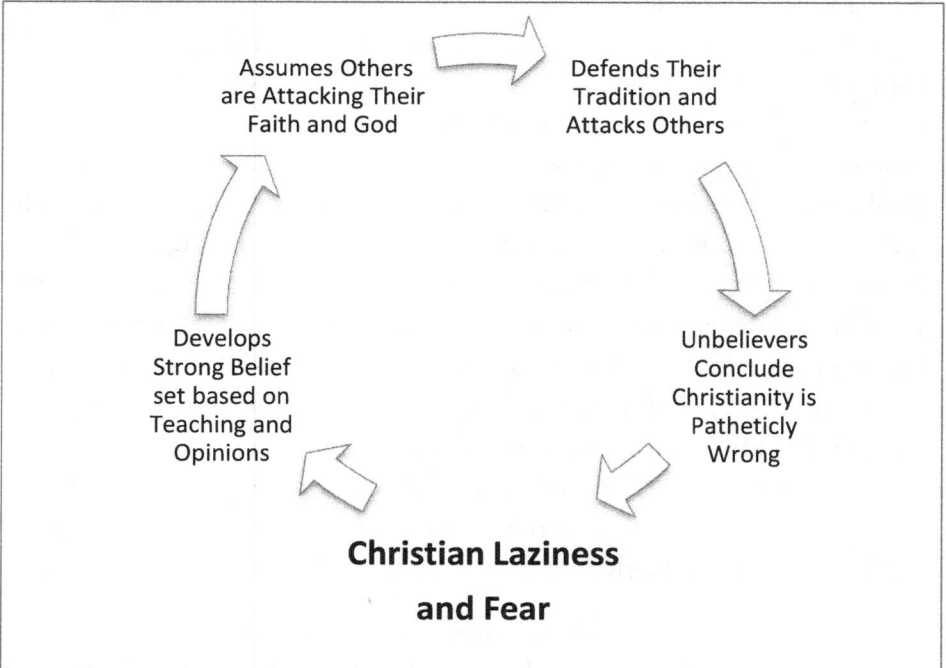

Assumes Others are Attacking Their Faith and God

Defends Their Tradition and Attacks Others

Develops Strong Belief set based on Teaching and Opinions

Unbelievers Conclude Christianity is Patheticly Wrong

Christian Laziness
and Fear

2

The Conflict in the Heavens

God's Dimension

We know so little of the Universe, of the vast heavens and of the spiritual dimension. We know so little of God's governing written requirements in the heavens and of what took place before humans, or of what is happening there now with its masses of angels, principalities, powers, rulers of darkness and spiritual hosts of wickedness. There are 100 million angels around God's throne alone. (Daniel 10:13,21; Zechariah 1:10-11; Ephesians 3:15, 6:12; Colossians 1:16, 2:15; 1 Peter 1:12; Revelation 5:11-14)

These extraterrestrial or extradimensional alien spectators are well aware of us living here on our little speck of earth, but faith is the only evidence that *we* have of *their* realms and abodes. By faith we can understand that past Eras were repaired by the invisible word of God.[1] (Hebrews 11:3) Similarly, scientists believe there is gravity and energy because of their evidence, even though they can't directly be seen and are not completely understood. (John 14:2)

Ezekiel got a fantastic glimpse into God's dimension of four amazing creatures with a human hand under each of their four wings. They fold two wings to cover their humanoid bodies as they fly in perfect wing-tip touching formation in the midst of bright fiery-amber whirlwind clouds of raging swirls of fire, with bursts of lightning flashing between and out of them. Their calf-like feet sparkle like gleaming bronze in fiery coals. These four creatures have four faces each; a man, a lion, an ox or cherubim, and an eagle. These faces may represent the four spiritual creations of God— Humans, Angels (cherubim/ox), Eagles (possibly spirit-enable birds of the heavens that fled in the Mesozoic Era), and Lions (Jesus is the Lion of the tribe of Judah). (Revelation 5:5)

The spirits of these creature are in four massive transparent-yellow wheels, each with internal spinning wheels, which stay beside them as they fly perfectly straight, without veering, in any one of the four directions of their four faces. They are encompassed all around with eyes, and their thundering wings sound like a tremendous waterfall. They stand still and fold their wings when a voice comes from above.

High above them a tremendously vast crystal stretches out as a sea of glass, and high over this the Lord God in human form sits on a translucent deep-blue throne, surrounded by a translucent green rainbow. God's waist up is like a deep-yellow amber engulfed in fire, and His waist down radiates as a bright, fiery rainbow. In front of God's throne burn the seven lamps of fire with His seven Spirits, and around Him on thrones sit twenty-four elders wearing golden crowns. This is eternity, where God dwells. (Ezekiel 1; 10; Revelation 4; Isaiah 57:15)

The Trinity

Ezekiel states, from his own perspective, that God has human form, but it is we who have God's form. Why does God refer to Himself as "Us" and "Our" in Genesis 1, "Let Us make man in Our image, according to Our likeness"? Because the Triune God made humans. God the Father made everything through Jesus the Son and His Spirit.

John mentions all three in one passage: "By this we know that we abide in Him, and He in us, because He has given us of His Spirit. And we have seen and testify that the Father has sent the Son as Savior of the world. Whoever confesses that Jesus is the Son of God, God abides in him, and he in God. And we have known and believed the love that God has for us. God is love, and he who abides in love abides in God, and God in him." - 1 John 4:13-16

God is one, and is also three: (1 x 1 x 1 = 1)

1) God the Father is love and dwells in unapproachable light.
2) God the Son is Jesus Christ the Lord and directly interacts with us in our physical dimension. Jesus lived in human form and died on the cross out of God's love for humanity. Jesus is like God's avatar for His physical creation, but He is also God, and is God's Son.
3) God the Holy Spirit is God's Spirit and gently motivates, comforts, teaches with whispers, is omnipresent, and is passively quenchable.

(John 1; 14:6-26; Ephesians 4:30; 1 Thessalonians 5:19; 1 Timothy 6:16; 2 Peter 1:21)

God the Father is known as the "Ancient of Days" or the "Lord of Hosts" in the Old Testament. God the Son was the "Angel of the Lord" and the "I AM" in the Old Testament, and was later born as Jesus in the New Testament, and is now known as the Lord Jesus Christ—

In Genesis 22:17, the Angel of the Lord tells Abraham, "I will bless you and multiply your descendants as the stars of the heaven and the sand on the seashore. Your descendant will take over and possess the gate of the hated adversary. Praised will be your descendant for all of Earth's nations."

In John 8, Jesus explains that He is from above, and that Abraham rejoiced in looking forward to His coming. The people ask Jesus, "You aren't even fifty years old. How can you say you have seen Abraham?"

Jesus answers, "Before Abraham was even born, I AM."

In Exodus 3:13-16, Moses asks the Angel of the Lord in the burning bush, "When I tell the children of Israel "The God of your fathers has sent me to you," and they ask, "What is His name?", what shall I say?"

God said to Moses, "I AM WHO I AM. Say to the children of Israel, "I AM has sent me to you.". The Lord God of your fathers, the God of Abraham, the God of Isaac, and the God of Jacob, has sent me to you. This is My name forever and is My memorial to all generations."

In Zechariah 1:12, the Angel of the Lord prays, "O Lord of Hosts, how much longer will You not have mercy on Jerusalem and the cities of Judah, which You were angry with for these seventy years?"

In John 17, Jesus prays, "Father, the hour has come. Glorify your Son so He can give glory back to you. You have given Him authority over everyone and He gives eternal life to each one you have given Him. This is the way to have eternal life—to know You, the only true God, and **Jesus Christ, the one You sent to Earth**. I brought glory to You here on Earth by completing the work You gave me to do. Now, Father, bring me into **the glory we shared before the world began**. May they have perfect unity so the world will know You sent me and that You love them as much as You love me. Father, I want these whom You have given Me to be with Me where I AM. Then they can see all the glory You gave me because You loved me even before the world began! Then Your love will be in them, and I will be in them."

(Genesis 16:8-13, 22:11-17, 31:11-13; Exodus 3:2-17; Judges 2:2, 13:9-23; Daniel 7:9-14; Zechariah 1; John 8:1-58)

Alice and E.T

A basic rule in writing movie scripts or books is that there has to be *something* normal people can relate to. Alice represents normality in the abnormal world of *Alice in Wonderland*. In the movie, *E.T. the Extra-Terrestrial*, the abnormal space creature E.T. is in a normal American suburb. But there is a *lot* going on in God's dimension that we don't yet know of, so it is difficult for God to communicate these things to us when we can't yet relate to them from our current perspective.

We are made in God's image and He loves us, so we can relate to God a little bit. We know a little of Satan. Like those living long ago who were only told a brief synopsis of what occurred in Genesis, God has just told us what we need to know for now.

For Trekkies and *Doctor Who* fans, God may now have some analogies to draw upon to explain more of it. But the Bible was written thousands of years ago to people who knew nothing of *Doctor Who* or *Star Trek*. So, for them, and for us, God just informed us of what we humans need to know for now of His dimension and the Universe.

Overview of The Conflict in the Heavens

God and His Son Jesus create the sons of God and Lucifer. After this, Lucifer and these sons of God shout for joy when Earth is created.

Lucifer watches God make the first five major Eras. At some point, Lucifer is lifted in pride in wanting to be like God and becomes a murderer. Lucifer loses access to the heavens and is cast to Earth and becomes Satan, or the devil, before Adam is made. Satan assumes the body of the serpent and deceives Eve into influencing Adam to disobey God. Satan then obtains the power of death over humans with this sting of sin, gains control of Hades and Paradise, and becomes the reigning death god of planet Earth. Satan leverages this to regain access to the heavens, and can again present himself before God. So, when God placed Adam and Eve in the midst of this vast spiritual conflict, God already knew this would all happen, and had already predestined a plan to deal with Satan, even before He had created Earth!

God is still executing His plan when Satan enters the body of Judas to betray Jesus about two thousand years ago. Jesus dies to wrest this power of death from Satan, and then takes back with Him to heaven all of the souls of believers who had been held hostage in Paradise.

Jesus has already won and defeated Satan. We are just waiting for the clock to run out as the massive influx of believers is currently being added to God's realm. Satan is presently concealing himself as an angel of light, and his followers as ministers of righteousness.

Satan and his angels have a place they can stay at in the heavens, but Michael and his angels cast Satan out of the heavens and back to Earth. Then, at the end of the Great Tribulation, Satan is cast into the bottomless Abyss for one-thousand years while Jesus refurbishes Earth and peacefully rules during His one-thousand-year millennial reign of planet Earth.

Earth becomes a near-perfect social and technological utopia with peace, prosperity and long-life spans. At the end of His millennial reign Jesus lets Satan back out, and Satan quickly causes havoc on Earth. God then sends out a fire that consumes the planet and its atmosphere, burning everything except Jesus and His believers. After this, God permanently casts Satan into the lake of fire, along with everyone who has been held in Hades, and then casts Death and Hades into the lake of fire and destroys them. In the very end, God makes all things new.

There is more on this in the chapter, "The Spirit and Super Body."

~~~

Years ago, my brother-in-law moved across the country to live close to us for a fresh start, and soon married a friend of ours. They were happily married and very much in love. Six weeks after their wedding he was fatally injured in a construction accident, leaving his nineteen-year-old widow deciding when she should end his life support.

I was with her when he died, and it was one of the most impacting events of my life. Later, well-meaning people told her, "Well, it was his time to go and God wanted him home," and "God needed him so He called him home." This really disturbed her, and she told me in tears, "I needed him more than God needs him!" I told her people should be careful to not blame God for what Satan might be responsible for, and that I saw the hand of Satan in it (Paul, Silvanus, and Timothy wrote that they wanted to come, "but Satan hindered us"). I also saw human error. God doesn't stop all of the bad things from happening, but God *can* bring good from them, and His Spirit can comfort and teach us, and Jesus *has* made a way for us to be reunited. In time, my sister-in-law healed and happily married again. (1 Thessalonians 2:18)

The Conflict in the Heavens

Jesus Christ the Lord

It was Jesus who gave life to **everything** that was ever created. He is from the beginning and was with God and He is God. (John 1:1-15)

"He is the image of the invisible God, the firstborn over all creation. For by Him all things were created that are in heaven and that are on earth, visible and invisible, whether thrones or dominions or principalities or powers. All things were created through Him and for Him. And He is before all things, and in Him all things consist."
- Colossians 1:15-18

"You are worthy, O Lord, to receive glory and honor and power; For You created all things, and by Your will they exist and were created." – Revelation 4:11

Jesus "was foreordained before the foundation of the world, but was manifest in these last times for you." - 1 Peter 1:20-21

Lucifer

Jesus created Lucifer as a son of the dawn, or a son of the morning. Lucifer shouted for joy when the foundation of Earth was laid—

"Where were you when I laid the foundations of the earth? Who laid its cornerstone, when the morning stars sang together, and all the sons of God shouted for joy?" (Job 38:4-7)

But afterwards Lucifer was lifted in pride, wanting to be like God—

"How you are fallen from heaven, O Lucifer, son of the morning! How you are cut down to the ground, you who weakened the nations! For you have said in your heart: 'I will ascend into heaven, I will exalt my throne above the stars of God; I will also sit on the mount of the congregation. On the farthest sides of the north; I will ascend above the heights of the clouds; I will be like the Most High.' Yet you shall be brought down to Sheol, to the lowest depths of the Pit. "Those who see you will gaze at you, and consider you, saying: 'Is this the man who made the earth tremble, who shook kingdoms, who made the world as a wilderness and destroyed its cities, Who did not open the house of his prisoners?'" - Isaiah 14:12-17 (Luke 10:18-19)

Did Lucifer shake kingdoms, make the world a wilderness, destroy its cities, and not open the house of his prisoners during the Mesozoic Era? Regardless of when or where it was, Satan fell from heaven because of it.

God revealed more of this to Ezekiel. The king of Tyre had supplied the gold and cedar for the temple that Solomon built, and he is an analogy of Satan in this account. Ezekiel's vision is of Satan's past—

"Thus says the Lord God: 'You were the seal of perfection, full of wisdom and perfect in beauty. You were in Eden, the garden of God; every precious stone was your covering: The sardius, topaz, and diamond, beryl, onyx, and jasper, sapphire, turquoise, and emerald with gold. The workmanship of your timbrels and pipes was prepared for you on the day you were created. You were the anointed cherub who covers; I established you; you were on the holy mountain of God; you walked back and forth in the midst of fiery stones. You were perfect in your ways from the day you were created, till iniquity was found in you.

<u>By the abundance of your trading you became filled with violence within</u>, and you sinned; Therefore I cast you as a profane thing out of the mountain of God; And I destroyed you, O covering cherub, from the midst of the fiery stones.'" - Ezekiel 28:11-16

Was Satan filled with violence during a fantastic Middle-Earth period of the Mesozoic Era? When God commanded the angel sons of the morning, is Satan the dawn that God caused to know his place by casting him out of heaven, when the wicked were shaken out of the extremities of the earth and their light was withheld? (Job 38:6-7, 12-15) Is Jeremiah 4:23-27 referring to the dark pre-human time when Earth became without form, and void, when the birds of the heavens fled, its cities were broken down, and Earth's atmosphere became so black it blocked all of the sun and star light? Was Lucifer involved in Earth's trembling destruction per Haggai 2:6? Could these Mesozoic Era inhabitants be the dead of the sea that are given up in Revelation 20:13? Suggesting some passages indicate that there may have been Mesozoic Era cities is about as crazy as Simon Episcupus teaching in the 1600's that he thought Genesis 1:2 indicates that there was an Era prior to ours. (For more information on this, read my book, *God and Humans*)

Jesus said that Satan was a murderer from the beginning, that there is no truth in him, and when Satan speaks a lie he speaks from his own resources, for he is a liar and the father of it. Jesus doesn't say when Satan became a murderer. Satan has drawn a massive one third of the angels to him, and at some point they will fight Michael the archangel and other angels in a war of the heavens.

Beelzebub, which means lord of the flies, or the dung god, rules over demons, but the origin of demons is not revealed. Satan might be Beelzebub, or may just have more authority than Beelzebub on Earth. Demons favor the sea, are associated with birds, and detest the bottomless Abyss that Jesus can command demons to go into. (Matthew 8:28-32, 12:24; Luke 8:31, 10:18; John 8:44; Revelation 12:3-12, 18:2)

God's Master Plan

God the Father knows the beginning from the end, since He inhabits eternity. No one can find out what God does from the beginning to the end, and only God from eternity knows all that will ever happen. (Exodus 3:14; Isaiah 57:15-18; Ecclesiastes 3:11; Colossians 1:16-17; Acts 15:18; Hebrews 13:8)

Before Adam and Eve, and all the way to our present time, there has been, and still is, this broader problem in God's realm involving Satan. God wants companionship and relationships with others. God is love, but God also wants peace, justice and order, and needs to deal with Satan. God creates humans in His image in Genesis 1, and they proliferate. It doesn't say if Satan had accused these humans of being blessed with copious amounts of self-control,[2] but when they need farming abilities to sustain their dense populations, God makes Adam.

God's plan to deal with Satan began way before He made Adam with the capability to choose to obey His instructions. God knew before they even took place of all the bad things that would transpire in our world. He knew Adam would rebel and sin, and that all of humanity would be held under Satan's power of death with this sting of sin. God already knew Satan would leverage Adam's sin to set up his own throne as the god of planet Earth with this power of death, and would again gain access to heaven. (2 Corinthians 4:3-5; Hebrews 2:14) God already knew of all the problems that Adam's sin would cause. God hates sin because it harms others, but especially because sin separates us from Him.

So, way before Adam was made or Earth was even created, God had foreordained Jesus to overcome Satan, spiritual and physical death, and sin. Sin is not *a* problem: it is *the* problem. To end sin is to ultimately end all human suffering. That is why, billions of years ago, God pre-planned, or predestined, His son Jesus to be a sinless genetic descendent of Adam, and to pay the price of death for Adam's sin that will cause death and sin to spread to all of humanity. God already knows the angels will minister to these humans. (Genesis 3:15; Romans 5:12-17, 8:29; Hebrews 1:13-14; Peter 1:20-21; Revelation 5)

God predetermined a way for us to be reconciled with Him, so all we have to do is believe in Jesus to protect our souls from judgment. God's foreordaining of Jesus resolves the problem of sin for both on Earth and in the heavens. God knew, long before He created Earth, that all believers will someday live with Him on a new, renovated earth.

All believers will have already chosen to serve God, and to reject themselves and Satan, by believing in God during their life here on Earth. You see, there is still this problem with other angels later rebelling against God, as Lucifer and his angles have. So, God will have humans, in their new, vastly superior physical bodies, judge the angels in the future. This puts a fix in place for dealing with future fallen angels.

> "Do you not know that we will judge angels? How much more, things that pertain to this life?" - 1 Corinthians 6:3

God starts executing His predestined plan. God knows the future because He dwells in eternity. He made time, and time consists in Him.

"Even from everlasting to everlasting, You are God." - Psalms 90:2

Adam's Disobedience

Genesis seems simple when it is understood from Adam's limited perspective, but we now know that Lucifer was cast to Earth, entered or assumed the body of the cunning serpent, and deceived Eve into influencing Adam to disobey God. (Revelation 12:3-9, 20:2)

Adam or Eve may have added in the additional "nor shall you touch it" to keep from being tempted by the fruit, since God said not to eat from the tree of the knowledge of good and evil, but said nothing of just touching it. This enlightenment of good and evil that Adam and Eve received went far beyond a mere understanding of consequences. After being deceived, desiring the fruit and disobeying God, they then saw good and evil from a supernatural perspective. Adam and Eve's eyes were opened and they received the perspective of clothed angels from the heavenly realm. No longer naive, they suddenly realized they were naked. This was a supernatural enlightenment of good and evil.

So, when God gives Adam a direct order to not eat from this tree, God already knows Adam will disobey and Satan will gain control over Earth with the power of death with this sting of sin, that Jesus will descend from Adam and overcome this power of death, and for thousands of years billions of humans will need to decide if they should accept or decline God's gift of eternal life, and that Satan and his angels will be destroyed in the end, along with Death and Hades—

"Now the serpent was more cunning than any beast of the field which the Lord God had made. And he said to the woman, 'Has God indeed said, 'You shall not eat of every tree of the garden'?'

And the woman said to the serpent, 'We may eat the fruit of the trees of the garden; but of the fruit of the tree which is in the midst of the garden, God has said, 'You shall not eat it, nor shall you touch it, lest you die."

Then the serpent said to the woman, 'You will not surely die. For God knows that in the day you eat of it your eyes will be opened, and you will be like God, knowing good and evil.'

So when the woman saw that the tree was good for food, that it was pleasant to the eyes, and a tree desirable to make one wise, she took of its fruit and ate. She also gave to her husband with her, and he ate. Then the eyes of both of them were opened, and they knew that they were naked; and they sewed fig leaves together and made themselves coverings. And they heard the sound of the Lord God walking in the garden in the cool of the day, and Adam and his wife hid themselves from the presence of the Lord God among the trees of the garden.

Then the Lord God called to Adam and said to him, 'Where are you?'

So he said, 'I heard Your voice in the garden, and I was afraid because I was naked; and I hid myself.'

And He said, 'Who told you that you were naked? Have you eaten from the tree of which I commanded you that you should not eat?'

Then the man said, 'The woman whom You gave to be with me, she gave me of the tree, and I ate.'

And the Lord God said to the woman, 'What is this you have done?'

The woman said, 'The serpent deceived me, and I ate.'"

- Genesis 3:1-13

Satan's Rule

Satan is the ancient serpent who deceives humanity, the great fiery red dragon and wonder in heaven who was punished and cast out of heaven to Earth with his followers, who gained control over Hades and Paradise with the power of death to become the reigning death god of planet Earth. (Romans 5:17; 2 Corinthians 4:4; Hebrews 2:14; Revelation 12:3-9)

This was all due to Adam's disobedience as a son of God. Satan is now the prince of the power of the air, the spirit that now works in the disobedient, and the whole world lies under his sway. Satan gained the power of physical death with this sting of sin, and the humans are now vulnerable, and their souls are in peril. (Matthew 4:9; 1 Corinthians 15:55-56; 2 Corinthians 4:4; Ephesians 2:2; Hebrews 2:14; I John 5:19; Jude 9; Revelation 12:9)

The fruit from the tree of good and evil wasn't magical, but symbolic. Their punishment came after they ate the fruit. It is like pushing the symbolic red button for launching a nuclear arsenal, and then wondering later how that little red button could be so powerful to have caused all of that. Sin was released and evil spread throughout the entire human race. Humans, made in God's image, were now living and relating to one another with this supernatural enlightenment of knowing good and evil. Because of Adam's disobedience to God, sin entered the entire world, and the dominion of death spread to all men, reigning even over those who had not sinned like Adam had. Adam is a type of Jesus, who later ended what Adam had started. (Romans 5:12-17)

Under the influence of Satan and his angels, and their newly found knowledge of good and evil, humanity rejected God and sinned.

It isn't relevant if we are related to Adam,[3] but that we live on planet Earth where Satan is a god and gained power over our human souls with this power of death. Each human spirit is given by God, not from any genetic relationship to Adam, so the spirits of genetically altered humans are under sin also. We now know good and evil after being born as human, and are now accountable, as the angels are. (Ecclesiastes 12:7)

Lucifer, who had rebelled against God and was cast out of heaven, now, as the god of Earth, again has access to God's realm. Satan, as he did with Job and Joshua, is now incessantly accusing people of things to God in heaven, and demanding justice upon us. (Revelation 12:10) God is planning for the long term, but it is His divine will (Luke 11:2) that there is now discord in His dimension, and in the heavens, at this time—

Satan opposes and accuses Job—

"Now there was a day when the sons of God came to present themselves before the Lord, and Satan also came among them.

And the Lord said to Satan, "From where do you come?"

So Satan answered the Lord and said, "From going to and fro on the earth, and from walking back and forth on it."

Then the Lord said to Satan, "Have you considered My servant Job, that there is none like him on the earth, a blameless and upright man, one who fears God and shuns evil?"

So Satan answered the Lord and said, "Does Job fear God for nothing? Have You not made a hedge around him, around his household, and around all that he has on every side? You have blessed the work of his hands, and his possessions have increased in the land. But now, stretch out Your hand and touch all that he has, and he will surely curse You to Your face!"

And the Lord said to Satan, "Behold, all that he has is in your power; only do not lay a hand on his person."

So Satan went out from the presence of the Lord." – Job 1:6-12

Satan opposes and accuses Joshua—

"Then he showed me Joshua the high priest standing before the Angel of the Lord, and Satan standing at his right hand to oppose him.

And the Lord said to Satan, 'The Lord rebuke you, Satan! The Lord who has chosen Jerusalem rebuke you! Is this not a brand plucked from the fire?'

Now Joshua was clothed with filthy garments, and was standing before the Angel. Then He answered and spoke to those who stood before Him, saying, 'Take away the filthy garments from him.' And to him He said, 'See, I have removed your iniquity from you, and I will clothe you with rich robes.'" – Zechariah 3:1-4

In the past the Lord solicitated input from those in His realm; they stood by Him and offered their advice; but in the end, thrones are set up for twenty-four elders, and 100 million angels will proclaim Him worthy and minister to Him. (1 Kings 22:19-23; Daniel 7:9-10; Revelation 4-5)

Free will, though it makes evil possible, is also the only thing that makes possible any love or goodness or joy worth having
– C.S. Lewis, Mere Christianity

The Savior

All of us, even high priests, need help, a redeemer, since Satan is now accusing believers to God day and night, or as it happened to Peter, is asking to sift us like wheat. (Luke 22:31-32; Revelation 12:10)

It is sin that keeps us from having a social utopia, and why all forms of human government, and space exploration, will have failure. Sin causes wars, crimes, social problems, selfish ambitions and injustices. But more importantly, sin separates us from God. Sin is not *a* problem, but it is *the* problem that troubles humanity everywhere. To end sin is to end human suffering. So, Jesus of Nazareth comes, God in a human body, and with power and the Holy Spirit, He helps others, healing all who are oppressed by Satan. (Acts 10:38)

In C.S. Lewis's book, *The Lion, The Witch, and The Wardrobe*, the boy Edmund sins under the trickery of the White Witch. The White Witch confronts the Lion and successfully argues that Edmund must die. But the Lion pays for Edmund's wrongdoing with his own life instead. However, since the Lion hadn't sinned, he comes back to life. The reason the Lion can pay for Edmund's wrongdoing and come back to life is because of a "deeper magic." The lion represents Jesus, who paid the price for our sins. (C.S. Lewis was led to the Lord by his friend, J.R.R. Tolkien, author of *The Hobbit* and *The Lord of the Rings*, who was also a believer in Jesus.[4])

The Lord, known on Earth as Jesus, knew, of course, of this "deeper magic". Satan had taken advantage of an existing law or requirement over humans because of Adam's sin. But Jesus bailed us out of that law and requirement by dying on the cross, so now all we need to do is ask forgiveness and believe in God to get God's gift of grace, a free pass to be with God and live forever physically.

Since Jesus had knowledge of good and evil, and was sinless, He conquered Satan and gained control over death—

"Because God's children are human beings– made of flesh and blood– the Son also became flesh and blood. For only as a human being could he die, and only by dying could he break the power of the devil, who had the power of death. Only in this way could he set free all who have lived their lives as slaves to the fear of dying."
– Hebrews 2:14-15 NLT

"But after Jesus died on the cross, <u>He wiped out the handwriting of requirements that was against us, and disarmed it, nailing it to the cross</u>. Then, 'having disarmed principalities and powers, He made a public spectacle of them, triumphing over them in it.'" - Colossians 2:13-15

After Jesus did all of this for us, He laid His right hand on John and said, "Do not be afraid; I AM the First and the Last. I AM He who lives, and was dead, and behold, I AM alive forevermore. Amen. And <u>I have the keys of Hades and of Death</u>." - Revelation 1:17-19

It's like Captain America bursting into a well-fortified stronghold, disarming the bad guys, rescuing the prisoners, and then triumphantly leading them out while holding the very weapons of death that were used to imprison them. Or a bit like Neo's control of the Matrix after his resurrection that rendered the Agents powerless.

Jesus made a public spectacle of them, triumphing over them in it. Since Jesus now holds <u>the keys of Hades and Death</u>, the gates of Hades, and Death, no longer spiritually prevails against believers, so our souls and spirits now skip Paradise and go directly to be with the Lord. (Matthew 16:18, 2 Corinthians 5:8)

We are not fighting against humans, but against spiritual crowds of wickedness in the heavenly places— against Satan and his angels, against the principalities, powers, and against those who rule the darkness of our time. (Ephesians 6:12)

Jesus, who is God, is also a direct genetic descendant of Adam. He lived a sinless human life and died to pay for all of humanities' sin. So now, any human who repents of their sin and gives up their own will, and accepts and submits themselves to God's will, is freely given God's Holy Spirit and the gift of eternal life by believing, and their names are not blotted out of God's Book of Life. Jesus paid the full price for Adam's original sin that afflicted all of humanity, and He will soon completely destroy Satan, Hades *and* Death.

Believers in Jesus can now say, "I am persuaded that neither death nor life, nor angels nor principalities nor powers, nor things present nor things to come, nor height nor depth, nor any other created thing, shall be able to separate us from the love of God which is in Christ Jesus our Lord." - Romans 8:38-39

All who dwell in the heavens now know of God's manifold wisdom and plan for believers— Paul said, "I was chosen to explain to everyone this mysterious plan that God, the Creator of all things, had kept secret from the beginning. God's purpose in all this was to use the church to display His wisdom in its rich variety to all the unseen rulers and authorities in the heavenly places. This was His eternal plan, which He carried out through Christ Jesus our Lord. Because of Christ and our faith in Him, we can now come boldly and confidently into God's presence." - Ephesians 3:9-12 NLT (Ephesians 4:7-10; Acts 10:45)

The invisible God made through Jesus everything that exists in the heavenly realms and Earth. Jesus is supreme over all creation, and existed before time or space or anything that was created. Everything was created for Jesus, and He holds all of creation together. Jesus made everything that we can see and everything we can't see, such as the thrones, kingdoms, mansions, rulers, and authorities in unseen worlds. God predetermined before Earth was even created that Jesus Christ the Lord would live on Earth as Jesus and die for our sins. God had Jesus purchase our freedom so He can forgive our sins and rescue us from the kingdom of darkness, and transfer us into His Kingdom. (Jeremiah 33:22; 2 Kings 22:13-28; John 14:2; Colossians 1:13-17; 1 Peter 1:20-21)

Satan's System of Hypercriticism

Satan is involved in drugs and immoralities, but also, in a truly more diabolical way, Satan subtly disguises himself as an angel of light, and his servants as ministers of righteousness. There many wicked hypocritical religious things they cozen humans to do in religion that are erroneously blamed on God. How more devilish of a way is there for Satan to fight against God, but to pose as God and influence people to do depictable things so that humanity blames God for them?[5]

Paul wrote, "I will continue doing what I have always done. This will undercut those who are looking for an opportunity to boast that their work is just like ours. These people are false apostles. They are deceitful workers who disguise themselves as apostles of Christ. But I am not surprised! Even Satan disguises himself as an angel of light. So it is no wonder that his servants also disguise themselves as servants of righteousness. In the end they will get the punishment their wicked deeds deserve." - 2 Corinthians 11:12-15 NLT

Satan, the god of this age, is blinding the minds of unbelievers to conceal the gospel so they can't see the light of the gospel that reveals the glory of Christ, who is the image of God. (2 Corinthians 4:3-4)

Jesus told the self-righteous poisonous snakes of His time, "If God were your Father, you would love Me because I came from God. I did not come for Myself, but God sent Me. Why can't you understand Me? Because you are not able to listen to My word. Your father is the devil, and you desire to do whatever he wants you to do. He was a murderer from the beginning, and does not stand in the truth because there is no truth in him. When he speaks a lie, he speaks from his own resources, for he is a liar and the father of it. But because I tell you the truth, you do not believe Me." (John 8:42-46; Jeremiah 12:2, 29:14, 38:24-26)

Satan's masquerade as a religious angel of light, and his followers as religious apostles of Christ, are highly successful schemes for blinding unbelievers' minds to Christ. Either of these two extremes can indicate that Satan or his apostles are influencing a church or religion—
1) Controlling legalism with misuse of scripture, requiring compliance with the leadership's doctrines, and devaluing of relationships.[6]
2) Broad permissiveness of conduct, and a vague reliance on scripture.

(Mark 8:15; Galatians 5:16-26; 2 Timothy 2:15-18; Titus 3; 1 Peter 1:14; 3 John 9-10)

Legalism is Satan's assault on God's wisdom and insight.[6]

Ignorance and stupidity give Satan his broad destructive power.

Actor Chris Pratt, of Guardians of the Galaxy and Jurassic World fame, while surrounded by large glorifying posters of himself in a pinnacling moment of his career during the MTV award of 2018, gave glory to God and pointed people towards Christ.[7] It was laced with comments I wouldn't want my kids to repeat, *but* it was appropriate for an MTV show, and MTV did not publicly object. Chris says he has a burden for young people and some may not like how he goes about it. (Luke 9:50) Chris said, "I would not be here...without my Lord and Savior Jesus Christ."[8] As Jesus said, if God is our Father, then we love Jesus.

Ironically, some religious folk took to the internet with accusations, insinuating Chris was an agent of Satan...— a tendency towards making judgmental accusations is Satan-like, not Christ-like. Jesus wants us to be impartial with others. To be partial is to be a judge with evil thoughts. Mercy triumphs over judgment. (Luke 9:49-50; James 2:1-14)

The Future

Michael is the great angel prince who watches over the Jewish people, and there are many angels in heaven who fight with him.

Satan, who is called the serpent of old, the great fiery red dragon, or the devil, has a place in the heavens that he can go to now with his wicked angels, the principalities and powers who rule in the darkness of our time. Satan is responsible for deceiving humanity. (Revelation 12:9)

In the future, during the Great Tribulation, a war breaks out in heaven when Michael and his angels fight against Satan and his angels. Near the end of this war, the place where Satan and his angels can go to in heaven is terminated, and Michael and his angels are able to cast Satan and his angels out of the heavens and down to Earth.

When Satan and his angels are finally cast out, a loud voice in heaven says, "Now salvation and strength and the kingdom of our God and the power of His Christ have come, because <u>the accuser of our brethren, who accused them before our God day and night, has been cast down</u>. They defeated Satan with the blood of the Lamb and the word of their testimony, and they did not love their lives to the death. **So be very glad, all you who dwell in the heavens**, but watch out, all you who dwell on the earth and are of the sea! For Satan is coming down to you in a great rage, because he knows his time is running out."

After Satan realizes he can't get back into the heavens, he and the angel Abaddon persecute Israel, because Jesus was Jewish, but the Jews take flight and hide. Satan knows the God of peace will crush him soon, and quickly causes millions of believers to be slaughtered. Jesus Christ soon comes back to Earth with His army in great clouds and defeats Satan. An angel then locks Satan up in the bottomless Abyss, and sets a seal on Satan so he can't deceive the nations for one thousand years.

The Lord then reigns for one thousand years on Earth. Near the end of the Lord's millennial reign, Satan is released from the bottomless Abyss and soon deceives all of the nations into attacking the Lord's holy city. Fire comes down from God and devours the attackers, and Satan is then cast into the lake of fire forever. All who rejected God will then be destroyed, and then finally Hades and Death are destroyed.

God will then descend in His incredible new city and dwell with Humans. There will be a new, fantastically beautiful Earth. (Daniel 9:27, 10:13,21, 12:1; 1 Corinthians 15:23-24; Jude 9; Revelation 9, 12:7-14; 20, 21)

The Importance of Jesus's Genealogy

God's foreordaining of Jesus for reconciling humanity to God was predestined even before He created Earth. It is God's will that this be done. (Matthew 6:10; 1 Peter 1:20-21; Romans 3:27-28, 4:4-5, 5:1-2, 8:29-30, 10:9-13, 11:32; John 3:16; Revelation 3:20, 5:1-14)

This is why Genesis 5:1 states, "This is the book of the genealogy of Adam," and why Luke gives Mary's biological genealogy of Jesus, to make it clear to us that Jesus is a sinless genetic descendant of Adam.

Matthew prophetically altered the royal genealogy of Jesus to give insight into Daniel's prophesy of Jesus, and symbolically provides six weeks of generations to point out that Jesus is the seventh generation, the Millennium Lord of the Sabbath.
(Matthew 1:11,17; Revelation 5; Daniel 9:24-25)

Adam's sin spread to all humans because of the supernatural battle for humans between Jesus and Satan, and by faith alone we know that Jesus satisfied these laws and written requirements in the spiritual realm to gain control of the souls in Paradise. (Colossians 2:13-14)

"When Adam sinned, sin entered the world. Adam's sin brought death, so death spread to everyone, for everyone sinned. For the sin of this one man, Adam, brought death to many.

But even greater is God's wonderful grace and his gift of forgiveness to many through this other man, Jesus Christ. And the result of God's gracious gift is very different from the result of that one man's sin. For Adam's sin led to condemnation, but God's free gift leads to our being made right with God, even though we are guilty of many sins.

For the sin of this one man, Adam, caused death to rule over many. But even greater is God's wonderful grace and his gift of righteousness, for all who receive it will live in triumph over sin and death through this one man, Jesus Christ.

Yes, Adam's one sin brings condemnation for everyone, but Christ's one act of righteousness brings a right relationship with God and new life for everyone. Because one person disobeyed God, many became sinners. But because one other person obeyed God, many will be made righteous. God's wonderful grace rules give us right standing with God, resulting in eternal life through Jesus Christ our Lord."
(Passages from Romans 5 NLV)

Accusations and Grace

Evil is hurting other people for enjoyment.

Evil is hurting innocent children and people to feel powerful.

Evil is having reckless regard for others, and hating them.

Evil is deceiving naive people to hold all human souls hostage, and then relentlessly making accusations against them.

~~~

Good is a superhero stopping a crazed robot from killing a child.

Good is stopping a bus full of innocent people from going off of a bridge that a villain has pushed with a semi-truck.

Good is helping others, even at great risk and peril to ourselves.

Good is being kind and considerate in small ways.

Good is stopping self-righteous hypocrites from stoning a woman to death for committing adultery.

Good is taking care of a poor man and paying for his medical care with no expectation of any benefit or recognition for doing it.

Good is self-sacrificing, giving for the good of others.

Good is having mercy and forgiving others.

Good is loving people.

Good is Jesus dying on the cross for the sins of the world, and then freely offering love, salvation and eternal life to everyone.

Good is God's grace, His undeserved goodness on all.

Only God is truly good. (Matthew 5:16,19:17; John 3:16; Revelation 12:10)

Understanding this is a supernatural enlightenment-

The Crucifixion by Gustave Doré

3

The Book of Life

Even if humanity progressed in knowledge to the point where we understood everything that there was to know about the Universe, even if we knew all of the purported knowledge of quantum physics and DNA as it is portrayed in *Star Trek* and *Star Wars*, it still wouldn't measure up to knowing just the foolish things of God, which are still wiser than all human wisdom. (Isaiah 40:12-15, 26, 55:8-11; 1 Corinthians 1:25)

God conceptualized the physics that we describe with the pure language of mathematics, and the Universe instantaneously[9] obeys His decrees and materializes. It is difficult for our tiny minds to comprehend a timeless dimension that is beyond God's precise laws of physics, beyond what mathematics can describe.[10,11]

Considering how vastly intelligent God is, does He even care about us? How do we compare to God? Consider the tiny microbes that God made to crawl on our skin and defend us from harm even before our human immunity defense system reacts.[12] Our microbes outnumber our human cells, yet since they are so miniscule they account for only about 3% of our body mass. Do you think much about them, or love them? How our microbes relate to us still isn't close to how we relate to God.

God dwells in an unapproachable light beyond the Universe that no one has ever seen, or can see. Like the galaxy inside the marble dangling from the collar of the cat in *Men in Black*, we are insignificant. We are also corrupt— try not showering for a few months. But, in spite of all of this, we are made in God's image and He loves and values us very much. (Genesis 1:26; John 3:16; 1 Corinthians 15:53; 1 Timothy 6:16)

We can live nice moral lives and help others the best we can. Some of the nicest people I know do not claim to be Christians, yet care for others at a deeper level than many Christians do.

However, in the very end, when we stand before God the Father, it doesn't matter how moral we were, or what good deeds we did, or how much we cared for others. He will just check for our names in the Lamb's Book of Life. Everyone's name was written in it since the foundation of the world, but some names are blotted out.

The names which are blotted out **are not** made known to God, and they are later cast into the lake of fire and die the second death. But if our name has *not* been blotted out, then Jesus will confess our name to God the Father in the end, and we become **eternally** known to God, from the beginning to the end, and are allowed in. Not getting our name blotted out of this Book of Life is the key for God letting us stay with Him. (Daniel 12:1; Matthew 7:23, 25:12, 25:41; Revelation 3:5, 20:12, 15)

Heaven may be like the dimension described in *The Forgotten Door*, by Alexander Key.[13] The people of this other dimension can read each other's minds, which is okay because they have no evil thoughts. They live peaceful lives in simple homes in a great climate and have plenty of fruits and vegetables to eat. They spend their time on art, visiting, and learning new things.

Intriguing glimpses of God's dimension, or the future heaven and earth, might also be seen in Akiane Kramarik's paintings. Akiane Kramarik's parents were atheists, yet she was led to God and became an amazingly talented artist at a young age. She painted her inspirations, or revelations, some depicting God's dimension, and her parents later became believers because of her faith. Her *Prince of Peace* painting, completed when she was eight, is very impacting.[14]

Other glimpses of God's dimension might be seen from the little boy's perspective in the book, *Heaven is for Real*.[15] He almost died, and in the weeks afterwards described seeing things in Heaven matching biblical concepts that many adult Christians don't understand. Maybe this happened and maybe it didn't. But his father wanted to know what Jesus looked like, and showed the little boy many paintings of Jesus. The little boy said Jesus didn't look like any of the traditional religious paintings of Jesus, until later when he saw Akiane's *The Prince of Peace* painting, and excitedly said, "Yes, that is exactly what Jesus looks like!"

The little boy tells of Jesus teaching the deep things of God, of Satan coming to heaven at times with fighting and conflict, and of time passing both very quickly and very slowly in heaven.

God says one day is as a thousand years, and a thousand years as one day. So, time is simultaneously both incredibly slow and incredibly fast in God's dimension. That is a difficult concept to grasp, God dwelling in eternity, knowing all things from the beginning to the end.

God is eternal and never changes. When Moses wanted to know the Lord's name, God replied, "I AM WHO I AM. Thus you shall say to the children of Israel, 'I AM has sent me to you.'" (Exodus 3:14)

Jesus Christ is the same yesterday, today, and forever. (Hebrews 13:8)

Jesus created all of the visible and invisible things in Heaven and Earth; all of the angels, thrones, dominions, principalities and powers. They were all created for Him. Jesus is before all of these things, and by Him they all consist. (Colossians 1:16-17)

God is timeless and inhabits eternity. (Isaiah 57:15)

God is from everlasting to everlasting. (Psalms 90:2)

"He has made everything beautiful in its time. Also He has put eternity in their hearts, except that no one can find out the work that God does from beginning to end." - Ecclesiastes 3:11

"Known to God from eternity are all His works." - Acts 15:18

> When a believer becomes known to God the Father, He has **eternally** known them, from eternity past to eternity future. But those who never believe are never known to God, so God will have **never** known them.

The Book of Life

Moses spoke of God's Book—

"Now it came to pass on the next day that Moses said to the people, 'You have committed a great sin. So now I will go up to the Lord; perhaps I can make atonement for your sin.' Then Moses returned to the Lord and said, 'Oh, these people have committed a great sin, and have made for themselves a god of gold! Yet now, if You will forgive their sin - but if not, I pray, blot me out of Your book which You have written.' And the Lord said to Moses, 'Whoever has sinned against Me, I will blot him out of My book.'" - Exodus 32:30-33

King David spoke of it—

"Your eyes saw my substance, being yet unformed.

And in Your book they all were written,

The days fashioned for me,

When as yet there were none of them." - Psalms 139:16

Paul and Timothy wrote of it—

"And I urge you also, true companion, help these women who labored with me in the gospel, with Clement also, and the rest of my fellow workers, whose names are in the Book of Life." - Philippians 4:3

The Apostle John wrote about this Book of Life in the future—

"He who overcomes shall be clothed in white garments, and I will not blot out his name from the Book of Life; but I will confess his name before My Father and before His angels." - Revelation 3:5

"Then I saw a great white throne and Him who sat on it, from whose face the earth and the heaven fled away. And there was found no place for them. And I saw the dead, small and great, standing before God, and books were opened. And another book was opened, which is the Book of Life. And the dead were judged according to their works, by the things which were written in the books. The sea gave up the dead who were in it, and Death and Hades delivered up the dead who were in them. And they were judged, each one according to his works. Then Death and Hades were cast into the lake of fire. This is the second death. And anyone not found written in the Book of Life was cast into the lake of fire." - Revelation 20:11-15

"But I saw no temple in it, for the Lord God Almighty and the Lamb are its temple. The city had no need of the sun or of the moon to shine in it, for the glory of God illuminated it. The Lamb is its light. And the nations of those who are saved shall walk in its light, and the kings of the earth bring their glory and honor into it. Its gates shall not be shut at all by day (there shall be no night there). And they shall bring the glory and the honor of the nations into it. But there shall by no means enter it anything that defiles, or causes an abomination or a lie, but only those who are written in the Lamb's Book of Life."
- Revelation 21:22-27

It is super important to do a very simple thing to prevent your name from being blotted out of the Book of Life that Jesus, the Lamb, has. If your name is blotted out, you will be tormented in Hades. Then, later, at the great white throne judgment, Jesus will say to you, "I never knew you, depart from me", and you will be cast into the lake of fire and either burn forever or just cease to exist, a second-death worst-case scenario with no possible escape. (Matthew 7:23, 25:41; Revelation 20:11-12)

Don't think in terms of living a good life. Although we are made in God's image, and God really does love us, there is really only one thing we can do to prevent our name from being blotted out of God's Book of Life. Knowing what is good, and doing good things, doesn't get us the gift pass and angelic transportation to God's Kingdom. To some degree, we all know what is "good" *and* what is "evil." (Romans 3:21-26)

At the end of our current Era terrible things happen on Earth. Even now some wealthy hedge fund managers can sense this "big event" is coming soon and they need to prepare for it. The problem they have is, once the "big event" comes, their wealth and food will be targeted by others. If their own guards turn on them, how are they to keep order? Explosive collars around their guard's necks to force obedience?[16] God has this time of tribulation at the end in hopes more people will repent. It is a time when the peace taken from humanity results in global civil unrest and violence, high food prices and famine, death, and when vast fires and horrible pollution affect a third of the entire earth and cause more deaths. In addition, Satan is cast out of the heavens and down to Earth, and there are even more horrifying tribulations. (Revelation 6-21)

God is thinking of how we humans stand on the brink of eternity. Having a terrible thing happen in the vapor flash of our life really is very insignificant if we end up living eternally on a new earth with God. Remember having an adult put antiseptic medicine on your cut when you were a kid, or having someone get a splinter out? It stings and is painful, but it feels better after a little bit and heals up, and is soon forgotten about. When considering our eternal destiny, having something horrible happen at the end of our very brief life becomes insignificant if our name isn't blotted out of God's Book of Life.

God *could* instantly destroy Earth's inhabitants, but instead He mercifully gives humans more chances to repent, even to the very end, in hopes that He can usher more humans into His new earth. God is thinking of where humans will end up for all of eternity when He allows these terrible things to happen during the Great Tribulation. Some do repent in the face of these tragedies, while others do not. (Revelation 9:21, 16:11, 11:13, 16:9)

"As I live," says the Lord God, "I have no pleasure in the death of the wicked, but that the wicked turn from his way and live. Turn, turn from your evil ways! For why should you die?" (Ezekiel 33:11)

You see, God is still trying to work something out for all of us humans, even to the very end, because He genuinely loves us. Like God having Jonah tell the Assyrians of Nineveh that He will overthrow them in forty days. But after Jonah warns them of their inevitable destruction, they all turn from their evil ways, so God relents and doesn't bring this disaster upon them. Jonah was very angry that the Assyrians were not destroyed, because they had been extremely cruel to Jonah's people. Jonah said he had expected "God would relent, since God is gracious and merciful, slow to anger and abundant in loving kindness, One who relents from doing harm." (Jonah 4:2)

God wants a relationship with each one of us, so He gives us the ability to choose and obey Him, which also allows for disobedience. All of our problems arise from knowing good and evil and being under this condition of sin, which separates us from God. So, God, who is love, even before creating Earth, predetermines the way of salvation so we don't have to be expelled from Him. (1 Peter 1:20-21)

I think the wise woman of Tekoah said it best. The back story on this wise woman is that King David, although he is a man after God's own heart and wrote Psalms and kills Goliath, he also commits adultery with his neighbor, Bathsheba. After David finds out he had gotten Bathsheba pregnant, he kills off her very loyal husband in a very sneaky way. God, of course, saw all of this and was displeased, and let David know he and his family will have a lot of conflict because of it.

This conflict begins with David's first-born son Amnon becoming consumed with love and yearning to have sex with his half-sister Tamar, but he can't because it's improper. A crafty man then explains to Amnon how he can create this situation so Amnon can finally have sex with her. It works, except Tamar tries to talk her way out of it, so Amnon just rapes her. Right afterwards, Amnon hates her so much that the hate with which he hates her is greater than the love with which he had loved her.

Then, Amnon tells her, "Arise, be gone!"

So she says to him, "No, indeed! This evil of sending me away is worse than the other that you did to me."

But Amnon won't listen, calls in his servant, and says, "Here! Put this woman out, away from me, and bolt the door behind her!"

Tamar's brother, Absalom, is infuriated when he finds out. But he carefully conceals his fury, and secretly plots for two years before finally killing Amnon for raping his sister Tamar.

King David punishes his son Absalom for this by banning him from the royal city. Three years later, King David's general, Joab, sees that David is really missing Absalom, so Joab enlists this wise woman from Tekoah to help persuade King David to let Absalom come back. This wise woman makes up a story about herself and her two sons to get King David to understand her situation, and then turns the table on David and says the same situation applies to him and Absalom.

At the end of these sordid events, the wise woman of Tekoah makes this very profound statement—

"For we all die, and our lives become like water spilled out on the ground, which cannot be gathered up again. But **God does not take life away; instead He devises ways to bring us back when we become separated from Him.**" (2 Samuel 13:1-14:14)

God devised a way to bring His banished children back to Him. This is why Jesus, God in human form, died for our sins. The fact is, we all get our names blotted out of the Book of Life, unless we do something. God wants us to do that something. He wants us with Him.

The human minds that are controlled by Satan are so passively dependent on their bondage that they fight to remain enslaved, and they are so blinded by Satan's deception that they often can't see this liberty that God is offering them. God wants us to turn from Satan's darkness to His light and receive forgiveness of sins, to be made holy by faith in Jesus. (John 8:34; Acts 7:57, 26:18; 2 Corinthians 4:4; Galatians 4:7)

Believing and calling out to God for help and forgiveness prevents our name from being blotted out of God's Book of Life, and we become eternally known to the eternal God Almighty! The Lord says, "Repent, and turn from all your wrong doing, so your sins won't be your ruin. Throw away all the wrong things you have done against Me, and get a new heart and a new spirit. Why should you die? I have no pleasure in the death of one who dies. Therefore turn and live!"
(Ezekiel 18 paraphrased)

Many of us live quiet peaceful lives and haven't done anything close to what David, Amnon or Absalom did. But we may have done a few of the things that are on God's list of what He really hates.

God specifically notes six distinct sins that He hates, and the seventh is one that God abhors—

1) Looking like we are proud
2) Telling lies
3) Killing innocent people
4) Thinking of wicked plans to harm others
5) Being quick to do wrong things
6) Telling lies to pervert justice and harm others
7) Doing or saying things to damage the good relationships of others.
   (Proverbs 6:16-19)

Even our own conscience can deceive us in what we believe to be true to the core of our being. The Lord searches the innermost intentions of our spirit. We will never measure up to God's standard.
(Jeremiah 17:9-10; Romans 4:5; I Corinthians 10:29; Colossians 2:16)

God will check with Jesus's Book of Life at the very end, and if your name is written in it, then Jesus will confess your name before God and His angels, and you will receive the free gift pass for eternal life. (Matthew 7:23,25:41; Revelation 3:5) It is the believing in God and repenting of our sinful nature that prevents our name from being blotted out—

Jesus said, "For God so loved the world that He gave His only begotten Son, that whoever believes in Him should not perish but have everlasting life. For God did not send His Son into the world to condemn the world, but that the world through Him might be saved. He who believes in Him is not condemned; but he who does not believe is condemned already, because he has not believed in the name of the only begotten Son of God. And this is the condemnation, that the light has come into the world, and men loved darkness rather than light, because their deeds were evil. For everyone practicing evil hates the light and does not come to the light, lest his deeds should be exposed. But he who does the truth comes to the light, that his deeds may be clearly seen, that they have been done in God." - John 3:16-21

"But, beloved, do not forget this one thing, that with the Lord one day is as a thousand years, and a thousand years as one day. The Lord is not slack concerning His promise, as some count slackness, but is longsuffering toward us, not willing that any should perish but that all should come to repentance." - 2 Peter 3:8-9

"We are made right with God by placing our faith in Jesus Christ. And this is true for everyone who believes, no matter who we are. For everyone has sinned; we all fall short of God's glorious standard. Yet God, with undeserved kindness, declares that we are righteous. He did this through Christ Jesus when He freed us from the penalty for our sins. For God presented Jesus as the sacrifice for sin.

People are made right with God when they believe that Jesus sacrificed His life, shedding his blood. This sacrifice shows that God was being fair when He held back and did not punish those who sinned in times past, for He was looking ahead and including them in what He would do in this present time. God did this to demonstrate His righteousness, for He Himself is fair and just, and He declares sinners to be right in His sight when they believe in Jesus."
- Romans 3:22-26 NLT

"If you confess with your mouth the Lord Jesus and believe in your heart that God has raised Him from the dead, you will be saved. For **with the heart one believes** unto righteousness, and with the mouth confession is made unto salvation. For the Scripture says, 'Whoever believes on Him will not be put to shame.' For there is no distinction between Jew and Greek, for the same Lord over all is rich to all who call upon Him. For 'whoever calls on the name of the Lord shall be saved.'"
- Romans 10:9-13

"Therefore He is also able to save to the uttermost those who come to God through Him, since He always lives to make intercession for them." - Hebrews 7:25

'Come now, and let us reason together,' says the Lord,
'Though your sins are like scarlet, they shall be as white as snow'
 - Isaiah 1:18

"For I am persuaded that neither death nor life, nor angels nor principalities nor powers, nor things present nor things to come, nor height nor depth, nor any other created thing, shall be able to separate us from the love of God which is in Christ Jesus our Lord."
- Romans 8:38-39

What was I comparing this Universe with when I called it unjust?
— C.S. Lewis

God says there *are* no atheists— "They know the truth about God because He has made it obvious to them. For ever since the world was created, people have seen the earth and sky. Through everything God made, they can clearly see His invisible qualities— His eternal power and divine nature. So they have no excuse for not knowing God. Yes, they knew God, but they wouldn't worship Him as God or even give Him thanks. And they began to think up foolish ideas of what God was like. As a result, their minds became dark and confused. Claiming to be wise, they instead became utter fools.

You may think you can condemn such people, but you are just as bad, and you have no excuse! Since you judge others for doing these things, why do you think you can avoid God's judgment when you do the same things? Don't you see how wonderfully kind, tolerant, and patient God is with you? Does this mean nothing to you? Can't you see that His kindness is intended to turn you from your sin?"
(Romans 1:20-22, 2:1,3-4 NLT)

> *If the thing loved is base, the lover becomes base*
> *- Leonardo Da Vinci*

Jesus said, "I AM the door. If anyone enters by Me, he will be saved, and will go in and out and find pasture. The thief does not come except to steal, and to kill, and to destroy. I have come that they may have life, and that they may have it more abundantly." – John 10:9-1

Merely realizing Jesus is the door is much different than opening that door and walking in. Jesus doesn't force His way into our heart, we have to decide to open that door. Jesus offers all humans the gift of spiritual rebirth into a new spiritual being who is supernaturally instilled with God's Holy Spirit. All believers can, and should, look forward to physically living forever with God in our new physical, refabricated superbodies on a new physical earth. (Isaiah 65:17; John 3:16; 2 Peter 3:13)

> *Is it not My ways which are fair, and your ways which are not fair?*
> *- The Lord*
> *(Ezekiel 18:29)*

The Abundant Life for Believers

Believers who used their talents to serve God and others will have their life's work of gold and silver purified in God's judgment—

"Now if anyone builds on this foundation with gold, silver, precious stones, wood, hay, straw, each one's work will become clear; for the Day will declare it, because it will be revealed by fire; and the fire will test each one's work, of what sort it is. If anyone's work which he has built on it endures, he will receive a reward. If anyone's work is burned, he will suffer loss; but he himself will be saved, yet so as through fire."
- 1 Corinthians 3:12-15

Selfish believers will have little to show for their life's work of wood, hay and straw after it is consumed in the heat of God's judgment of their actions. They will be like a wheat plant bearing few kernels with little benefit to others, but their soul and spirit will be saved since their name wasn't blotted out of God's Book of Life.

For an abundant life in Christ

Jesus is our rock and the protector of our faith. We know we will live eternally with God and can live confidently since we have been spiritually reborn as children of God. So, we should diligently build on our foundational faith and the peace we have made with God, and grow in Christ by availing ourselves of God's undeserved goodness.

First, **desire moral excellence** to break the deliberate bad habits and lustful desires of our body and mind by learning to walk carefully as a child of God in His light. We can now take these sins that burden and so easily trip us up to God, since we now have the undeserved privilege of God's love pouring into our hearts.

Reverence God's word and be glad to learn His truth and wisdom and walk in it. God's insights protect us, and also weaponizes us to defeat Satan's subtle strategies— we aren't fighting humans, but against evil rulers and authorities from the unseen world who are mighty powers in this dark world, and against evil spirits in the heavenly places.

Find mature spiritual mentors who can encourage us, and meditate on the huge crowd of witnesses throughout the Bible as examples of faith for how we should conduct our own lives and what decisions we should make. Open yourself up to God's Spirit and His leading.

We can **run with endurance** the race God has set before us by keeping our eyes on Jesus, our champion, who endured such a brutal death and public humiliation from evil self-righteous people, but is now seated beside God. So, don't get tired and give up, since you have not yet given your life in your struggle against sin! We *can* reap the harvest of living right when we are trained in His ways. How often should we pray? Always. We can't overdo praying. God wants to hear from us all of the time. He always enjoys hearing from us and wants to help!

After we **learn to live self-controlled moral lives**, we need to take care to not be lifted in pride, because when the trials in life come, and they will, our pride will bring us down. But, Jesus is there to lift us up on our feet as many times as we ask. We should really be glad when our problems arise, because it is through patiently enduring them that we grow in our faith and our character grows stronger. The burden Jesus places on us is light and easy. Our soul will rest when we make our requests known to Him, learn to trust Him by carefully reading God's word, and walk in harmony with Him. We can not only *stand* with God's help in the times of our trials, but *remain* standing.

We should **have patience during our trials** because it is the very problems in our lives that reveal the weaknesses in our spirit, the hidden faults of our heart that God can help us with to develop our strength of character. These trials are the times that God is healing our spirit, so don't make light of the Lord's divine discipline, or give up as He corrects, because He does this out of His love in wanting us to share in His holiness since we are His children. This shows He really does love and care for us! He is the Father of our spirit, and this is why He wants to help us with our painful problems; to unburden us, heal us and give us peace. So, get a grip with your tired hands, strengthen your weak knees, and mark out a straight path for your feet! When we call out to God our Father for help, we will not fall, even when we become weak and stumble, because God will strengthen us. So, we should not resent our trials, but rather be glad when they happen, keeping in mind as we endure them that one day we will be with Christ.

If we stop growing in Christ and stagnate in mere self-controlled morals, our growth becomes stunted. We then fall into the subtle, damaging, and unfortunately all too common snare of self-righteousness and the pride of life.

As soon as we get our act together and start living a clean life for the Lord, the self-righteousness that is utterly against God can slink in if we begin to look down on others. This pride of life allows poisonous roots of bitterness to creep in and grow to corrupt us and those we know.

God's Spirit is glad to help us with our self-righteous bias and prejudices, whether they are personal, political or religious; we will not be disappointed as God unburdens us further and gives us more peace! We can also avoid drifting into this evil self-righteous attitude of looking down on other people by **reaching out to help others**, and make this the tenor of our lives in looking after and encouraging others to receive God's undeserved goodness. We need to work at living a holy life in peace with others, especially with those who do not know the Lord, in hopes that they someday will. We should share His gospel of peace with those we live with, and be genuinely concerned for others out of the hope that is in us. Our hope is our guarantee of living eternally with God. What we do in this life is investing for all of eternity, so we should look forward to our future with God and **live godly, self-sacrificing lives** with genuine love and concern for others.

When asked, we should always be ready to gently and respectfully explain our hope and future with God. We know **God loves us** because the Holy Spirit pours in and fills our hearts with His love.

(Psalms 19; Proverbs 11:2, 24:16; Matthew 11:30; Romans 5:1-5; Ephesians; Philippians 4:6; Hebrews 12; James 2:1-9; 1 Peter 3:15; 2 Peter 1:5-9)

To Fill my Spirit with God's Love

Desire and pray for moral excellence to heal my mind and body

Harmonize my spirit with God's Word and learn how to live

Have self-control and patiently keep practicing what I learn

Jesus will lift me up on my feet as many times as I need

Always be ready to explain the reason for my hope as a believer

Patiently endure trials while God is healing my spirit and character

Remember I will soon be with God, so avoid the pride of life

Help others– Get rid of my prejudices and be genuinely concerned

Let my words and inner thoughts be acceptable in your sight, Lord

Life Choices

Cold Immorality	Abundant Life	Hot Legalism
Desires of Body	Walking with God	Pride of Life
Stupidity	God's Truth	Reasoning Away
Overly Wicked	Eyes on Jesus	Self Righteousness
Leaven of Herod		Leaven of Pharisees

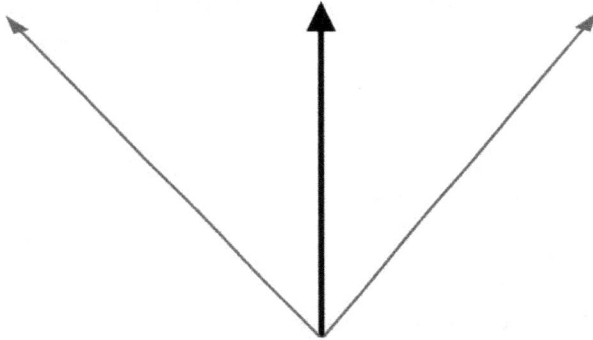

Fear God and Avoid Both Extremes

(Ecclesiastes 7:16-20; Mark 8:15; Galatians 5:16; Titus 3:8; Hebrews 12:2; 1 John 5:3)

Find out How God wants Me to Live → Seek God's Will for my Life

Walk with God in Peace and Humility

Desire Moral Excellence

Abundant Life of a Believer

OUR HEART

God designed our heart to be our will and intellect, the place for our innermost thoughts and feelings for everything that is in us. In our heart we decide to believe or turn away from God, we commune with ourselves, reason, ponder and understand. From within our heart comes our plans, integrity, joys, sorrows, and the troubles of our mind. Our heart allows us be in awe, merry, cheerful, merry or haughty, overwhelmed, humble or proud, depressed or glad, disquieted, strong or weak, desire, fail, turn back, meditate, rejoice, sorrow, praise, tremble and faint with fear, be unaware and deceived, stupid, bitter or conceited, or hardened against God and others. Our heart, whether it is weak or strong, greatly affects our imaginations and thoughts and what we do. Our heart becomes desolate when our spirit is overwhelmed. What we treasure comes from within our heart. Our spouse should be a seal on our heart. The wise in heart can have low or high IQ's.

No one has a clean heart, and we lack the ability to make our own heart pure. From within our heart comes evil thoughts of murders, adulteries, immoralities, despising others, lusts, naughtiness, perversion, and hypocrisy– which gives us a double heart of deceit and mischief. We can deceitfully steal the hearts of others. Our heart is evil from our youth with its snares and nets. We can turn our heart away from the Lord, or incline our heart to the Lord. We can be slow of heart to believe, or harden our heart and not hear the Lord with an evil heart of unbelief. The fool, regardless of his IQ level, doesn't seek to understand and says in his heart there is no God, and just wants to discover the many devices within his own heart. Satan snatches God's Word away from the hearts of those who hear, but don't understand it.

God's heart grieves when our heart is evil. We do evil if we don't prepare our heart to seek the Lord. We have to protect and keep our heart with all diligence, because out of it flow the issues of life. With our heart we believe to righteousness, and with our mouth confession is made for salvation. We don't have to let our heart be troubled— we can believe in Jesus, understand with our heart, and be converted with our faith. The Lord comes close to those who have a humble and broken and contrite heart. He sends His Spirit into our hearts, and we cry, "Daddy, Father!" God's Spirit dwells in our new adopted heart to comfort, teach and bless us.

We find rest for our soul when we humble ourselves and call out to the Lord and let Him know what is in our heart, and pray for Him to know our thoughts, when we set our heart to understand and purpose to walk in truth with a willing heart and mind to serve God with all our heart and soul, considering what great things He has done for us. We *can* praise and serve Him with a perfect heart and do His will.

When our heart burns within us for the Lord, and we ask with words and mediations that are acceptable in His sight, and prepare our heart to understand, He hears the desire of our humility. When we are not inclined toward our own understanding, but trust in the Lord, we allow His peace to rule in our heart. He gives us a spirit of revelation in knowledge and wisdom to walk in His statues and keep His judgments. He enlightens our understanding to know what His will and calling is.

The Lord searches our heart and already knows what is in our spirit. He perceives our thoughts and knows our hidden counsels; the secrets of our heart are known to Him. We can tell others what is in our heart, but the Lord already understands our innermost thoughts, imaginations, deceits, griefs and gladness. God's Spirit discerns the intents of our heart, and can remove sorrow from our heart.

When we love our own heart, we commune with the Lord to seek His counsels of knowledge, wisdom and instruction so He will apply our heart to understand His will for our life. Our heart motivates us to willingly serve the Lord. We should consider what is in our heart— sometimes when our heart indicates we should do things *we* think are good, or bad, we should put these aside to obey the will of the Lord. The Lord can give us an enlarged heart of kindness and wisdom to perceive and understand His will, and the motives of others, to turn hearts towards Him. Sometimes we should settle in our heart to not mediate beforehand what we will say to others, but ask God to have His Spirit speak from what our heart is filled with, like fruit that shows what kind of tree it is from. The Lord knows the hearts of all humans, and can move our heart to understand and speak His words. The Lord calls us to love Him with all of our heart and soul and mind and strength.

Heart verse highlights are in the back of this book under references.

This HEART study is based on the HEBREW leb- will and intellect (3820); lebab- will, intellect and feelings (3824); sekviy- mind (7907); GREEK kardia- will, intellect and feelings (2588); sklerokardia- hardness of heart (4641).

Strongs numbers are provided for Englishman/Reverse Concordance searches.

Precepts for Marriage

God made marriage a foundation of human relationships from the very beginning. Both men and women need love, respect, admiration, spending time together, doing things for each other and physical contact. Since marital conflicts arise from men and women prioritizing and valuing their needs very differently, God gave some foundational principles to help each couple understand the other's perspective so they can have a great marriage.

Men Crave Respect

Men want to be the superhero swooping down in their ingeniously self-created suit of armor and saving the day, as a smile plays on the lips of their admiring, and impressed, love interest. They also want love quite a bit, and a secure relationship, and some adventure. But mainly they require respect. A man loves a woman who is in awe of him.

Men want things to run smoothly, and be able to provide for their family without fear of going in need. Deep in their spirit, they desire to be a secure provider.

Women Crave Love

Women want to be passionately in love with their soul mate. No matter what happens in life their bonds of love will never be severed, no matter what tragedies befall them, or tempests in life beset them, they will always have their soul mate's love to count on, and they will always be loved and cherished and feel very secure in their love for each other. They also like having fun, being admired and complimented, but they require love. A woman respects a man who loves her deeply.

Deep in their spirit women want a sheltered nest to raise their family in without fear, and a secure and close relationship with their husband.

Marriage Conflicts

All marriages have conflicts, but it is how we respond that makes the difference— Be quick to hear, overlook offenses, slow to speak, slow to anger, pursue peace, and speak the truth in a loving way.

Always respond kindly, even to criticisms, and pray during conflicts.

We seldom regret using kind gracious words

(James 1:19; Proverbs 19:11; Ephesians 4-5; I Peter 3:9-12; Colossians 3:8-12)

Relationship Choices of the Heart

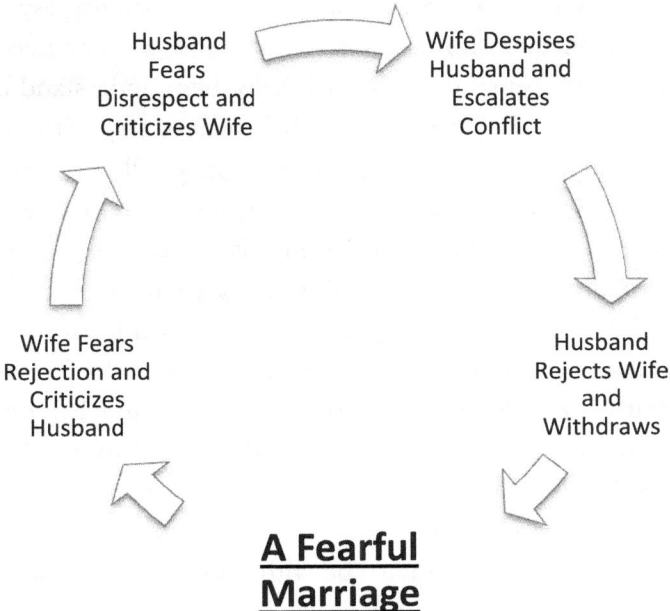

Wife is in Awe of Husband and is Harmonious

Husband is Confident- He is Devoted and Cherishes

Wife is Secure- She Admires and Respects

Husband Deeply Loves Wife

A Great Marriage

Husband Fears Disrespect and Criticizes Wife

Wife Despises Husband and Escalates Conflict

Husband Rejects Wife and Withdraws

Wife Fears Rejection and Criticizes Husband

A Fearful Marriage

Precepts for Raising Children

The good and bad examples set by parents are often perpetuated by their children for several generations. An amazing thing can happen when someone dedicates their life and actions to Christ– the cycles of destructive generational habits can be selflessly broken in love for their own children, and they can in turn give their children a big advantage.

A big advantage for what? Do we simply want other people to admire our parenting so we feel good about ourselves? Do we just want our children to admire, love and respect us, or is it that we just don't want to worry later on about what bad things our adult children might do next?

Our motive and goal for raising kids should be to equip them to love the Lord, help others, and be productive people in our society and church, whether it be as a spouse, raising their own children, or in a career. We rightfully evaluate others based on their level of unselfishness, so shouldn't we live altruistically as an example for them? (Hebrews 12:5-11)

More than anything, children are prone to follow the example their parents set, regardless of what is said or taught.

God gives some workable principles for raising kids in a harmonious, peaceful and pleasant home—

Young Children

Young children are so impressionable that their parents, especially their father, imprint on them how they will view God, so they need to know they are loved and feel secure. This will help them understand later in life that God loves them, and be secure in their relationship with God.

An angry parent is destructive, and unintentionally teaches them that God is angry and vindictive and causes pain, and so should be avoided.

An absent parent teaches them God is distant and not approachable.

A lazy parent teaches them God doesn't care what they do.

Young children need training in self-control, and learn to be adept at listening to instructions. This skill set will invaluably help them later in life without their ever realizing it. It also makes for a much more peaceful home. Children who learn to behave and take care of things don't require "kid-proofed" homes, and are able to engage their intelligence in more productive ways than with emotional conflicts. Children who exercise self-control at a young age are a joy to be with, rather than a source of stress for their parents, and for family and friends. (Ephesians 6:1-4)

Rather than teaching children to obey only after there is ten minutes of angry escalating conflict, teach your kids to obey with one calm request so they are pleasant to be around. Play the game of obedience—They have to carefully listen so they can instantly obey what you quietly instruct them to do. Make it challenging, and compliment them for compliance. Make it fun and stop while they are still having fun so they look forward to it next time. After they learn to walk, instill work ethics into their character by showing them how to pick up trash and sweep. Heap on the compliments. They *want* to feel valued and contribute to the welfare of the home. Having them help takes longer to get a job done, but they will become an invaluable help to you and others later on.

Set an example of being respectful, kind and considerate. Being unduly critical of other children can teach them to be cynical, so it is often better to just remove them from overly hostile environments.

Children need protection from exposure to harmful physical contact, substances and videos which can fester into hurtful life-changing habits that haunt them deeply as struggling adults. Children need clear boundaries, and they need to know "why" as they get older.

Children need protection from other children at times— schools and close-knit churches can create damaging hardships for kind children who are repeatedly subjected to the cruelty of other children who haven't learned how to be kind to others. (Proverbs 1:7, 3:11-12, 6:6,20, 10:4-5, 12:10-11,24, 13:4,20, 14:26, 20:7, 22:6, 27:10, 28:13, 29:17; Colossians 4:6, James 1:20)

Older Children

Older children need to learn more of God's principles, and develop their personal relationships, work ethics and how to manage money. They especially need to know the reasons why and understand the consequences, so they can see the importance and value in what is taught.

Learning the wisdom in Proverbs will be a tremendous asset to them later in life. Read Proverbs regularly, and act them out with little skits so it is fun and instructional. It will impart life-long wisdom and vital life principles. Teach them God is our "daddy." (Galatians 4:6)

God gave each child their unique spirit and soul and personality. Parents should help them discover their purpose, and teach them how to pursue God's work in their life. Children are going to learn, whether it is from their parents, friends or others. If parents don't have the initiative to teach them, then they will learn from others.

Self-disciplined scholars are a by-product of having good work ethics. Pay them for doing some work, and help them manage their money by allowing them to waste it on junk. After they soon tire of their cheap toys, then casually talk with them afterwards, with the broken toys in sight, about saving money for things that last. This way, as they get older, they already know the value of money and don't waste it. Teach them about budgeting, the pitfalls of credit card debt, the benefits of good credit, new car taxes and depreciation, and pre-paying home mortgage principle.

Allot generous and regular amounts of **quantity time** to be with them so those invaluable little talks can naturally arise in conversations.

Young Adults

Emerging young adults crave to be acknowledged and respected. God wants them to become independent of their parents and dependent on Him, to care for themselves and others, to have their own family. Their desire for independence should be nurtured with respectful guidance and life lessons about the pitfalls in life, how to avoid making stupid mistakes, relationship skills, and how to be interdependent– to have others they look to for advice besides their parents. Encourage them to pursue God and relationships with others of good influence. (Ephesians 2:3, 6:4)

Young adults struggle if they weren't taught God's principles in relationships, work ethics and handling money when they were young.

Young adult anger and cold rejection becomes manifest in children who lacked parental love, had poor examples, or were not taught self-control. Their attitude is fueled by a rejection of their parent's failures, so disrespectfully ordering them around as if they were still young children will just bring resentment. Asking them to do things and explaining the benefits of compliance will produce much better fruit in the relationship. It's never too late for parents to change and ask forgiveness for their own failures. Prayerfully repentant parents are much more respected by young adults than parents who fearfully contend to justify themselves.

Parent's Pledge– I will love the Lord with all my heart and strength. God's word will be written in my heart so I can diligently teach the ways of the Lord to my children by telling of them as we sit in our house, as we walk and drive, at night when I tuck them in, and in the mornings. Lord, direct what I do and let Your words be as a guiding headlamp on my forehead, and written on the walls of our home. (Deuteronomy 6:5-9)

Communication Choices

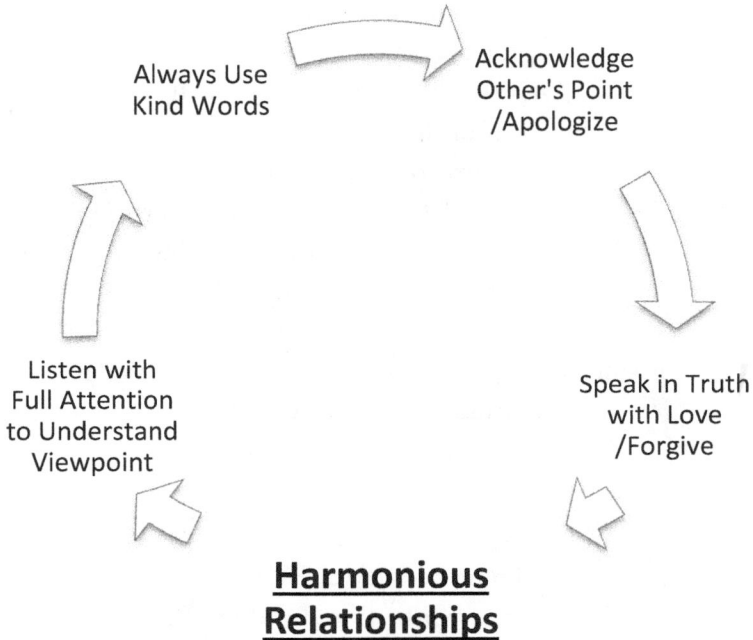

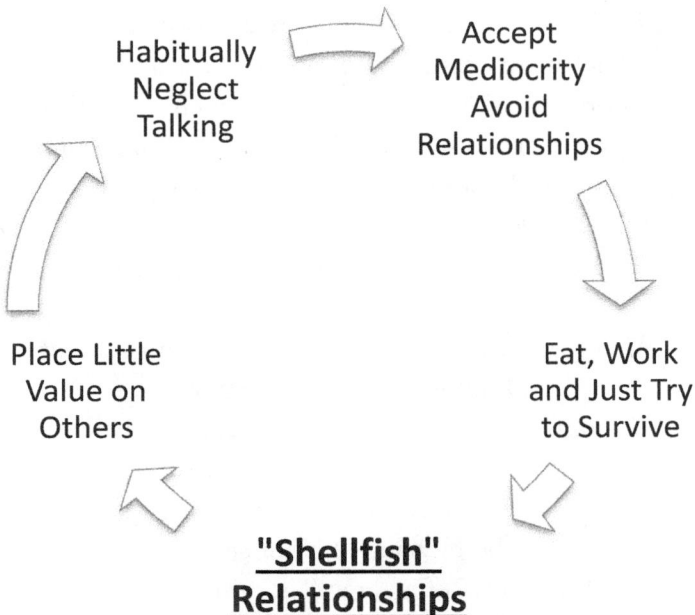

Always Use
Kind Words

Acknowledge
Other's Point
/Apologize

Speak in Truth
with Love
/Forgive

Listen with
Full Attention
to Understand
Viewpoint

Harmonious Relationships

Habitually
Neglect
Talking

Accept
Mediocrity
Avoid
Relationships

Eat, Work
and Just Try
to Survive

Place Little
Value on
Others

"Shellfish" Relationships

Psalms 19 – a poem of David set to music

The Cosmos declares splendor
God signing with His own hand
the arc of heaven above
Day after day pours out speech
Night after night shows knowledge
No words or language is heard
A voice streams musical words to Earth
Saying the brilliance of the sun was set within coverings
like a bridegroom at his wedding
rejoicing as an athlete running a race
Rising from horizon, revolving to horizon edge
Nothing hides from the heat

The Law of the Lord is Integrity
Converting the Soul
The Testimony of the Lord can be Trusted
To make Wise the simple
The Instructions of the Lord are Right
Cheering the Heart
The Commands of the Lord are Pure
Enlightening the Eyes
Reverence for the Lord is Pure and lasts Forever
The Judgments of the Lord are True and Fair
more desirable than gold, even much fine gold
sweeter than honey, even honey in the honeycomb
And your servant is warned within
keeping them is great reward
Who understands hidden moral mistakes?
Cleanse me!
Also from deliberate sins keep back your servant
Don't let them dominate me!
Then, free from fault, and innocent of rebellion
let the words of my mouth
and meditations of my heart
be pleasing in Your sight
O Lord, my Refuge, my Rock, my Redeemer

4

The Spirit and Super Body

Akiane Kramarik painted imagery of space and the earth that she may have received as a divine revelation. One is of her sanctuary.[14] I suspect, like me, she sees heaven as living in our new physical bodies on our newly renovated earth with fantastic streams and waterfalls, fruit trees, and astonishing colors we will see in the ultraviolet and infrared spectrums.

I did a rough calculation of how many acres an average sanctuary might be for each believer. Starting with the total acreage of our existing planet (there will be no seas or mountains), and guessing at 6 billion total believers, yields an average of twenty acres per sanctuary, if God's fantastic new city is orbiting overhead, as it seems to say.

Since our new physical bodies will be like Jesus had after rising from the dead, we may also be able to fly, go through walls, teleport, and telepathically communicate. Jesus will teach us amazing things, and there will be delicious fruit to eat. No roads, cars, gas stations or dentists, just our sanctuary homes and the Holy City. There will be perfect gender equality between males and females. (Matthew 22:30)

After 4.7 trillion peaceful years, everyone will know each other really well, and because there is no longer any sin, this is a good thing.

God, in His infinite love, freely offers us a gift pass to eternity. If we accept, then, Jesus said, "My Father will send you the Helper, the Holy Spirit, in My name. He will teach you everything and bring to your mind everything that I have said. I will leave you with my supernatural Peace, so do not let your heart be troubled or afraid." (John 14:23-27)

Believers connect to and communicate with God via the Holy Spirit. God's Spirit bonds with our human spirit after we believe, and we are then spiritually reborn as children of God. Our spirit's deep intentions influence our heart's decisions, and our soul's emotions and thoughts.

The thoughts of our soul and the decisions of our heart are closely entwined with the intentions of our spirit, but God's living and powerful Word can discern this difference between our thoughts and our intentions. (Proverbs 4:23; 1 Thessalonians 5:23; Hebrews 4:12)

Soul Overview

The Hebrew naphash and Greek psuche refers to our soul. Our soul is entwined with our spirit, and they depart from our body after death.

Our living soul contains our personality, thoughts and knowledge, our emotions and memories, our feelings, loves and hates, what we lust for and loathe, enables us to feel elated or sad, to deceive, desire and enjoy. Our soul also interfaces with the five senses of our body, and directs our actions. Our soul communes with our spirit, heart and physical body. Our soul reacts to what our spirit seeks.

We pour out our soul's emotions from the depths of our spirit— We complain of our soul's bitterness from our spirit's anguish, our soul desires what our spirit seeks, our soul is pleased with what our spirit judges to be good. (1 Samuel 1:15; Job 7:11; Isaiah 26:9; 42:1; Matthew 12:18)

Spirit Overview

The Hebrew ruwach and Greek pneuma refers to our spirit, or to evil spirits, angels, or to God's Spirit. It is our spirit that interacts with the supernatural, whether it be God's Spirit or unclean evil spirits.

Our spirit is our inmost part that motivates us at deep, sometimes subconscious, levels and inspires our soul's feelings and thoughts. Our spirit drives our loves and hates, and influences our conscience.

Our spirit's intents influence our heart's faithfulness or instability, impels our desire for excellence or mediocrity, to be content or sojourn.

Our soul and mind contain knowledge, but our heart and spirit embody wisdom, insight and understanding. God is Spirit, so we must worship God with our spirit in truth, not in soulish emotional worship. (1 Samuel 1:15; Job 7:11; Isaiah 26:9, 42:1; Matthew 12:18; John 3:5-7, 4:23-24, 14:23)

The spirit of each believer is uniquely reborn spiritually when it bonds with God's Spirit, who upgrades our understanding and connects us to God's 3.0 spiritual network. (Genesis 3:22; 1 Corinthians 6:16, 13:13)

Analyzing the hundreds of Bible passages regarding naphash, psuche, ruwach, pneuma, leb, lebab, and kardia, and what Jesus revealed of them, yielded the Human Spirit, Heart, Soul and Body Diagram ⇒

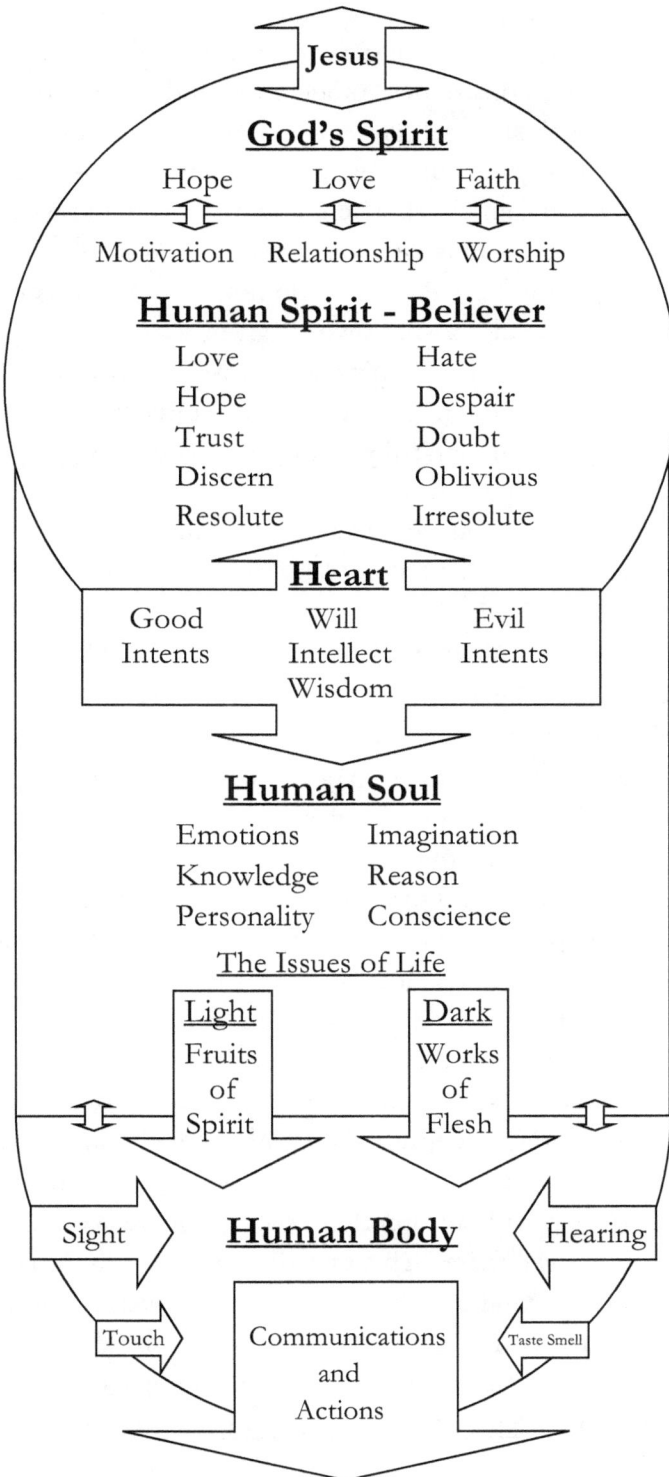

Jesus

God's Spirit

Hope	Love	Faith
Motivation	Relationship	Worship

Human Spirit - Believer

Love	Hate
Hope	Despair
Trust	Doubt
Discern	Oblivious
Resolute	Irresolute

Heart

Good Intents	Will Intellect Wisdom	Evil Intents

Human Soul

Emotions	Imagination
Knowledge	Reason
Personality	Conscience

The Issues of Life

Light Fruits of Spirit	Dark Works of Flesh

Sight   ## Human Body   Hearing

Touch   Communications and Actions   Taste Smell

The benefits of seeking God's will and walking in harmony with His Spirit are receiving and having love, satisfaction, peace, patience, kindness, goodness, consistency, moderation and self-control. There is certainly no law against these! (Proverbs 4:23; Galatians 5:13-26)

Jesus said, "The wind blows where it wants to. You can hear the sound of it, but you cannot tell where it comes from and where it goes. So it is with everyone who is born of the Spirit." (John 3:8)

"When we tell you these things, we do not use words that come from human wisdom. Instead, we speak words given to us by the Spirit, using the Spirit's words to explain spiritual truths. But people who aren't spiritual can't receive these truths from God's Spirit. It all sounds foolish to them and they can't understand it, for only those who are spiritual can understand what the Spirit means.

Those who are spiritual can evaluate all things, but they themselves cannot be evaluated by others. For, 'Who can know the Lord's thoughts? Who knows enough to teach him?' But we understand these things, for we have the mind of Christ." - 1 Corinthians 2:13-3:1 NLV

Unbelievers can't hear God's Spirit of Truth because they are tuned in to Satan's spirit of deception, so they speak from Satan's viewpoints. God's living Spirit in believers is greater than this deceptive spirit— we have the mind of Christ and can understand this deception. We can tell if someone is listening to this spirit of deception by seeing if they can understand God's Spirit of Truth. (1 Corinthians 2:16; 1 John 4:4-6)

There is an empty place in our human spirit for God's Spirit to enter in and bond with us and dwell so we become one with God. Since an unbeliever doesn't have God's Spirit, this place is empty, unless an unclean spirit resides there. An unclean spirit may subtly help in divining stock market prices, assist an unbeliever to charismatically run a large church or corporation, or depress them. (Acts 16:16; 1 Corinthians 11:14-15)

If an unclean spirit leaves and comes back to find an unbeliever's spirit is swept clean with an orderly life, it can go get seven even more wicked spirits to dwell there. This may drive the person into crazed and violent acts, so they wind up in prison or a mental ward. This is how it is in our wicked generation. (Matthew 12:43-45; Acts 19:16)

Believers have a rebirth of their *spirit* which impacts their *soul.*

The *spirits* of *unbelievers* are in one of these two circumstances ⇒

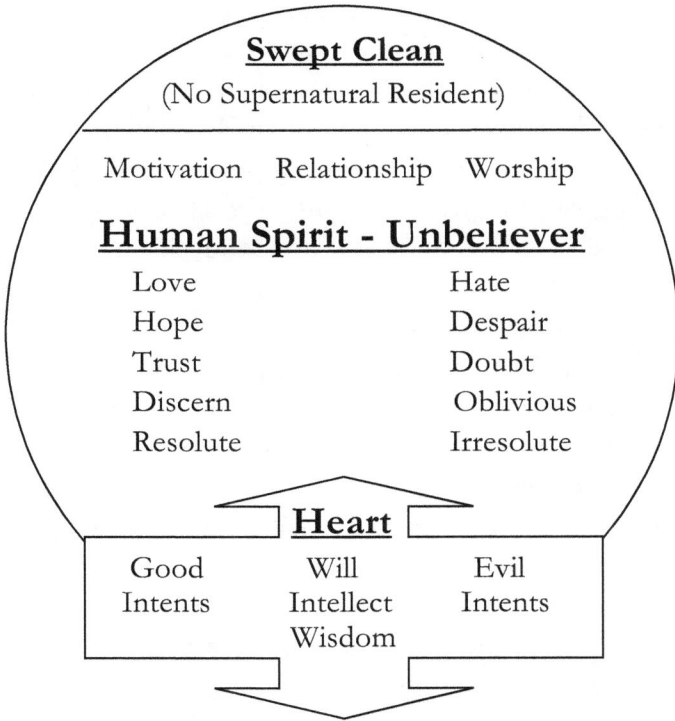

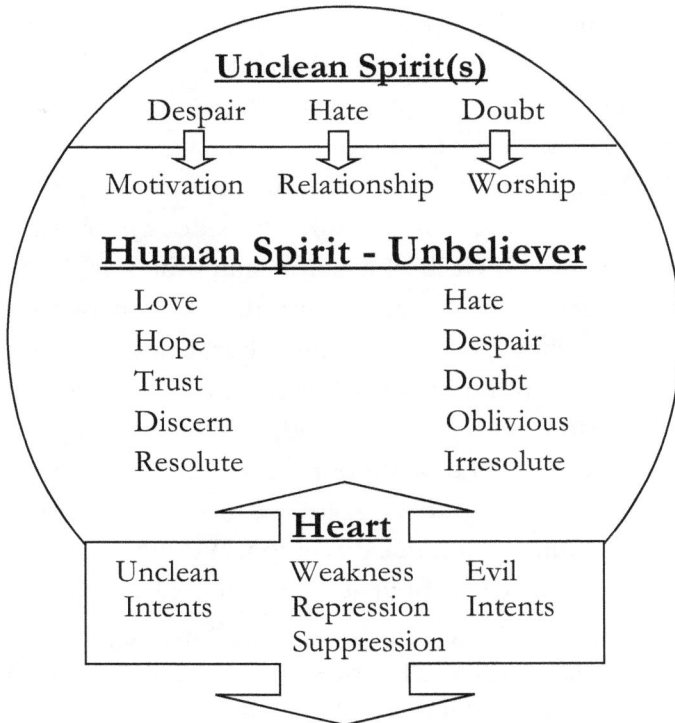

SOUL

Our soul is our life that dwells within our physical body. The Lord breathed life into Adam and he became a living soul. The Lord makes all human souls, and living animal souls, and in His hand is the soul of every living thing and all human lives. When our physical body dies, our human soul and spirit goes to be with the Lord, or to Hades.

Our body exists so our soul has a place to reside, our soul is like our heart's life blood. Our soul has conscious thoughts, emotions, desires, impulses, pleasures or displeasure, sorrow, depression, grief, hate, love, and adversity. It can be enticed, angry, or satisfied. Knowledge of wisdom is a sweet reward to our soul. Our soul becomes humbled with fasting. Our physical body lusts and wars against our soul, so our soul can be unstable. Our heart interacts with and directs our soul.

Doing right preserves our soul, such as having mercy, but cruelty troubles our soul. Our soul can convince and win over the thoughts of others. We honor other people with our soul in what we do. Our soul can be physically drawn to others, and lust for others. Controlling what we say keeps our soul's thoughts from trouble— being friends with an angry man and learning his ways sets a snare for our soul's thoughts.

Jesus gave His life, His Soul, for those who believe. Our lives, our souls, are saved by believing God's word, but the Lord's Soul has no pleasure in those who draw back. When we seek to find our life we lose our soul, but when we lose our life for Christ we find our soul. The Lord's Soul is well pleased when we love Him with all our heart, soul, mind and strength, and walk before Him in truth with all our heart and soul. Our soul, our life, rests with God. We can magnify the Lord with our soul. Sometimes we should not consider the thoughts in our soul's mind because God's Spirit will help us say the right thing. Our soul lives as the Lord lives. God can heal our soul after we sin. We convert our soul by putting God's instructions into our mind.

We should desire God with our soul's thoughts, pour out our thoughts to God, and lift our soul, our life, to God, wait upon Him and look to the Lord with delight in expectation. We should bless and praise the Lord with the thoughts of our soul and with what we do.

Soul (Life) verse highlights are in the back of this book under references.
This SOUL study is based on the Hebrew naphash (5315) and Greek psuche (5590).
Strongs numbers are provided for Englishman/Reverse Concordance searches.

SPIRIT

God made our spirit, and all life, with the Spirit of His Word. God's Spirit conceived Jesus in Mary's womb, descended on Jesus like a dove, led Jesus to a desolate place to be tempted by Satan, and raised Jesus from the dead and brought Him back to life. God's Spirit is a gift, the Spirit of Truth that is now in the world speaking through us, directing our actions, and is totally immersed within a believer's spirit.

In God's hand are the spirits of all humanity. Our spirit perceives, rejoices, and purposes with intent what our heart wills to do. Our spirit can have quietness, trouble or distress. The sorrow of our heart can cause our spirit to be broken and changed for the better. When our spirit is overwhelmed, our heart becomes desolate. When our heart melts, so does our spirit. We can have a double portion of spirit to double our life's work. Our spirit can sustain us in illness, but we can also have a wounded spirit. Humans can have spirits of grief or heaviness, and spirits of immorality or guileless, judgment, jealousy, courage, anger, sorrow, anguish, grief, corruption, trouble, faithfulness, patience, irritation with understanding, haughtiness, pride or humility. We can have an excellent spirit of understanding. **When our spirit revives, it renews our soul to stir our heart to action.**

Even if our spirit is willing to do good, our bodily desires can overcome our spirit. Our self-control arises from our heart ruling our spirit, but the foolish follow their own spirit. What we say motivates our spirit to act— wholesome words give life, but perverseness is a breach in our spirit. Fools utter all that is in their spirit, but the wise are very careful of what they say of it. We should take heed of our spirit so we are not treacherous or deceitful to our loved ones. People can change our spirit for good or for bad. A stubborn and rebellious generation have wavering spirits with hearts that are not right with God. Our spirit can turn against God, or our spirit can be contrite from a broken heart before God. No human has power over their own spirit to retain it after death— our body dies when our spirit leaves us.

God created the Universe and doesn't want sacrifice or good works, but desires, and greatly values and delights in, a gentle, humble and contrite spirit who trembles at His word. When we believe and turn to God in repentance and ask Him to create a clean heart and renew a right spirit within us, then He casts away all of our transgressions and gives us a new heart, and puts in us a new spirit so we can learn to walk in His ways. God's Spirit falls on us when we hear God's Word and we believe by faith, not by what we do. We are then born of God's Spirit and can enter His Kingdom. God sends the Spirit of Jesus as a gift down from heaven into our hearts and adopts us, and we cry, "Daddy, Father!" God's Spirit dwells within our spirit, and we know we are children of God! Our body is now the temple of the Holy Spirit which lives in us, and we are not our own. God's Spirit searches our spirit and knows our inner heart and mind, and dwells in our innermost parts. God's Spirit is life, not a spirit of fear, but an earnest spirit of power and love that is spread in our hearts, a spirit of freedom and of a sound mind. God's Spirit is written in our hearts and in our spirit.

We were bought with the death of Jesus, so we should glorify God in our body and spirit, which now belongs to God, and serve God with our new spirit. But we still have our old spirit... We should seek to please our spouse with our spirit, and conduct our lives and actions consistent with God's Spirit so we have a life of peace. With our soul we desire God, and with our spirit we seek God and learn to do what is right. We can live according to God's Spirit because we dwell in Him and He in us. God's Spirit comforts and guide us into all truth and gives wisdom, and directs our actions when we consciously know it, but we can decide in our heart if we will follow it. God's Spirit in us doesn't speak with enticing words of human wisdom, but with the power of God, and gives us a change of heart and a spirit of holiness, fills us with joy, and gives us discernment and strength. When we don't know how to pray, God's Spirit communicates for us with God in ways that we cannot express. We can build our faith by earnestly praying in God's Spirit, and to always keep praying. The Word of God is God's Spirit, and is how He communicates with us. We call Jesus the Lord with God's Spirit.

When we suppress and quench or tempt God's Spirit by rebelling or saying bad things, it vexes and grieves God's Spirit within us. When our spirit is overwhelmed with troubles, and our soul refuses to be comforted, we can tell God about this and commune with God in our heart and search for Him diligently with our spirit, and God will direct us. He blesses us when we are poor in spirit, and does not despise a broken and a contrite heart! God's Spirit regenerates and renews our spirit, and purges our conscience so we can serve the living God!

When we put aside our old spirit and renew our God-given spirit, we are filled with God's Spirit. Then the Lord pours in us His Spirit of wisdom so we can know, understand and discern His will. God's Spirit gives life and freedom, and refreshes our spirit, so we should keep walking in and doing what His Spirit leads us to do, and not immoralities or legalism, which are destructive. The things done for our bodies are corrupt, but what is done with God's Spirit lasts forever.

God's One Spirit gives gifts of wisdom, knowledge, faith, healing, miracles, discernment and languages. The Lord gives spirits of grace, discernment, craftsmanship, art, strength, inspiration, stirs our hearts to action, teaching and counsel, strengthen us, and gives an understanding spirit. His Spirit of discernment can direct and revive us. His Spirit can be on us to preach liberty from captivity to the brokenhearted.

Reverence of the Lord makes us quick to understand.

The Spirit of God dwells in all believers. We are all joined in unity as a temple of God to the Lord in One Spirit. So, we should endeavor to seek peace with others. When we despise other believers, we despise God, who gave us His Spirit. Other believers can refresh our spirit, and we can be with others in spirit even when we are not with them. Our spirit can be restless when other believers are troubled. We should stand together with other believers and worship God with our spirits, we are *all* in God's Spirit, and strive together for the faith of the gospel. The gospel comes in power in God's Spirit. Treat others who sin in a spirit of meekness, and develop habits of earnest prayers for ourselves and others so that God will preserve our whole spirits and souls and bodies to be blameless when our Lord Jesus Christ comes. Our new spirit groans for a new, refabricated body, but our spirit is perfected by God, so we should not be shaken in our spirit or mind by words, but allow God's Spirit to give us grace, wisdom and His knowledge.

God makes His angels spirits of flaming fire, and sends them out to minister to us. God can make unclean or strange spirits pass from the land, or send a perverse or lying spirit into the midst of a country and cause them to err in everything they do. People can be vexed with unclean spirits, but God's Spirit can control these evil spirits.

Spirit verse highlights are in the back of this book under references.
This SPIRIT study is based on the Hebrew ruwach (7307) and Greek pneuma (4151).
Strongs numbers are provided for Englishman/Reverse Concordance searches.

Spirit DNA

A tiny planted seed that grows into a productive new plant is like a believer's spirit and soul that grows into a powerful new body. Jesus said, "A grain of wheat is just one grain of wheat, but if it gets into the ground and dies, it will grow and produce many grains."

A modern allegory to a single grain of wheat is DNA, but a special sentient spirit DNA that interfaces with our soul's emotions, memories, thoughts, imagination, conscience and personality.
(Job 7:11; Isaiah 42:1; Matthew 12:18, 13:30; John 12:24-26; I Corinthians 15:37-45; 1 Thessalonians 5:23; Hebrews 4:12; John 12:24)

Jesus will protect our soul if we believe in God and ask in repentance for help and forgiveness. We become spiritually reborn when God's Holy Spirit enters us and bonds with our spirit's DNA. The Holy Spirit then dwells inside each believer, comforting and teaching us. This gift can't be earned by simply living a good life and trying not to sin. Only the indwelling of God's Spirit protects our spirit DNA, and guarantees that we will someday receive new physical bodies. A believer's spirit DNA returns to God after the death of our body because it is now inseparable from God's Spirit. But the spirit of an unbeliever remains corrupted by sin after death because they lack the power to resurrect themselves, and their soul and spirit later returns to God at the end for judgment.
(Ecclesiastes 12:7; Revelation 20:4-5,11-15)

Since God is God of the living, not of the dead, God will someday match each believer's soul and spirit to an incredible new physical body.
(Matthew 13:30; Mark 9:42-44, 12:27; Romans 3:23, 8:23; 1 Corinthians 15:35-58)

Our soul is designed to dwell in and interface with a physical body, so after death our soul and spirit will desire another one. Jesus will transform us when He is revealed, and we will acquire powerful new spiritual bodies of majestic splendor. We don't really know what our new bodies will be like, but we do know that our bodies will be like His.
(Matthew 22:29-32; Luke 24:31-39; Acts 1:9; 1 Corinthians 15:37-44; I John 3:2)

But, before we get our new physical superbodies, what exactly happens to our soul and spirit after our corrupt physical bodies die? Where is Paradise, Heaven, Hades and Hell? Why did Jesus have to die on the cross, and what changed afterwards? Where did souls go before Jesus died on the cross, and where do they go to now? Who controls Hades– Satan or Jesus? Or Abaddon?

Overview of the Spirit Investigation

Where souls and spirits have gone, and go to now, depends on the crucifixion and physical resurrection of Jesus.

Before the Death of Jesus Christ: All souls went to a domain in the lower parts of Earth. This domain is split in two by a deep fissure, with Hades on one side and Paradise on the other. Hades is unpleasant and Paradise is pleasant. When Satan gained the power of death, he gained control over this domain as the god of this world. Abaddon is in Hades. The souls of believers became trapped in Paradise and had to wait for Jesus to retroactively die for their sins to rescue them. God wanted to get His people out of Paradise, permanently.

Death of Jesus Christ: Jesus died and went down and emptied out Paradise, and brought with Him all of these souls up to heaven. The souls in Hades were left behind to wait for their final judgment of being cast into the lake of fire, which hasn't happened yet.

After the Resurrection of Jesus Christ: Believers now skip Paradise and go directly to heaven to be with Christ. The souls of those blotted out of God's Book of Life are still being added to Hades.

End Time: Abaddon is cast into the Lake of Fire. Later, those in Hades are brought up and judged. God checks the Lamb's Book of Life, and everyone's name that has been blotted out is cast into the lake of fire and to their second death, which is either ceasing to exist, or burning forever like Satan and the false prophet. Those with Christ will be here on the newly renovated earth with no mountains or seas.

The Spirit Investigation

Before the Death of Jesus Christ

King Saul is in a time of great distress and uncertainty. God won't answer him, so King Saul breaks his own law and asks a witch to call up the spirit of Samuel to get his advice. The soul of Samuel rises from the ground. Samuel is annoyed with Saul for disturbing him—

"After Samuel died and they lamented and buried him, Saul put all the mediums and spiritists out of the land. Then the Philistines gathered and encamped at Shunem. So Saul gathered all Israel together and they encamped at Gilboa. But when Saul saw the army of the Philistines, he was afraid and his heart trembled greatly.

Saul inquired of the Lord, but the Lord did not answer him by dreams or the Urim or by the prophets. Saul said to his servants, 'Find me a woman who is a medium so I can ask her.'

His servants said, 'In fact, there is a woman who is a medium at En Dor.'

Saul disguised himself by putting on other clothes, and went with two men at night to the woman. He asked her, 'Please, conduct a séance for me, and bring up the one I will name to you.'

The woman said, 'Look, you know what Saul has done, how he has cut off the mediums and the spiritists from the land. Why are you laying a snare for my life, to get me killed?'

Saul swore to her, 'As the Lord lives, you won't be punished.'

So the woman asked, 'Who shall I bring up for you?'

He said, 'Bring up Samuel for me.'

When the woman saw Samuel, she cried out, and said, 'Why have you deceived me? For you are Saul!'

King Saul said, 'Do not be afraid! What did you see?'

The woman said, 'I saw a spirit ascending out of the earth.'

Saul asked, 'What is his form?'

She said, 'An old man with a mantle is coming up.'

Saul perceived it was Samuel and bowed with his face to the ground.

Samuel said, 'Why have you <u>disturbed</u> me by bringing me up?'

Saul answered, 'I am deeply distressed; for the Philistines make war against me, and God has departed from me and does not answer me anymore, neither by prophets nor by dreams. So I called you so you can reveal to me what I should do.'

Samuel said: 'Why do you ask me, seeing that the Lord has left you and become your enemy? The Lord has done what I told you He would do, the Lord has torn the kingdom out of your hand and given it to your neighbor, David, because you did not obey the Lord. The Lord will deliver Israel and you into the hand of the Philistines. Tomorrow, you and your sons will be with me.'" - I Samuel 28:3-19

Samuel's soul looked like him, and could still see, hear, speak, and remember. Where did Samuel's soul rise from, and go back to? Jesus explained where this was with His story of a rich man in Hades who sees poor Lazarus in Paradise. This also offers a plausible reason for why Samuel was annoyed with Saul for disturbing him—

"There was a certain rich man who was clothed in purple and fine linen and fared sumptuously every day. But there was a certain beggar named Lazarus, full of sores, who was laid at his gate, desiring to be fed with the crumbs which fell from the rich man's table. Moreover the dogs came and licked his sores. So it was that the beggar died, and was carried by the angels to Abraham's bosom. The rich man also died and was buried. <u>And being in torments in Hades, he lifted up his eyes and saw Abraham afar off, and Lazarus in his bosom.</u>

Then he cried and said, 'Father Abraham, have mercy on me, and send Lazarus that he may dip the tip of his finger in water and cool my tongue; for I am tormented in this flame.'

But Abraham said, 'Son, remember that in your lifetime you received your good things, and likewise Lazarus evil things; but now he is comforted and you are tormented. And besides all this, <u>between us and you there is a great gulf fixed</u>, so that those who want to pass from here to you cannot, nor can those from there pass to us.'

Then he said, 'I beg you therefore, father, that you would send him to my father's house, for I have five brothers, that he may testify to them, lest they also come to this place of torment.'

Abraham said to him, 'They have Moses and the prophets; let them hear them.'

And he said, 'No, father Abraham; but if one goes to them from the dead, they will repent.'

But he said to him, 'If they do not hear Moses and the prophets, <u>neither will they be persuaded though one rise from the dead.</u>'"
- Luke 16:19-31

Jesus confirmed Paradise is a real place just before He died, when one of the criminals hanging next to Him impiously said, "If You are the Christ, save Yourself and us!"

The other criminal rebuked him, saying, "Do you not fear God, even after you got the death sentence!? We deserve death, but He has done nothing wrong!" Then he said to Jesus, "Lord, remember me when You come into Your kingdom."

Jesus replied, "I assure you, <u>today you will be with Me in Paradise</u>."

The thief had a short stay in Paradise, leaving within 48 hours to depart with Jesus.[17] (Luke 23:39-43)

After Bathsheba's affair with King David, she delivered a baby boy, who became very sick. David wept and fasted in hopes that the Lord would relent and make the baby well. But after the baby died, he said, "I fasted and wept when the child was alive, because I thought, 'Who can tell if the Lord will be gracious to me so the child will live?' But now that he is dead, so why should I fast? Can I bring him back again? <u>I will go to him, but he will not return to me</u>." (2 Samuel 12:23)

Where did David and the baby go after they died? The only place mentioned is Paradise (Bathsheba later had another son, Solomon, who was incredibly wise and wrote Song of Songs, Ecclesiastes, and most of Proverbs, so God brought good from this ugly situation).

<u>Death of Jesus Christ</u>

Christ went down and emptied Paradise of its captive souls, taking them back with Him so they could finally go to heaven—

Jesus said, "I led captivity captive, and gave gifts to men." In other words, after Jesus died on the cross, He went into the heart of the earth and rescued all of the believers who were being held captive in Paradise, those who had died after Satan gained control of death, and Jesus led these captives out and up to heaven. Now, Jesus freely gives His gift of His Spirit to any who believe and accept this undeserved goodness—

"But to each one of us grace was given according to the measure of Christ's gift. Therefore He says: "When He ascended on high, He led captivity captive, and gave gifts to men." (Now this, "He ascended" - what does it mean but that He also first descended into the <u>lower parts of the earth</u>? He who descended is also the One who ascended far above all the heavens, that He might fill all things.)" - Ephesians 4:7-10
(Psalms 68:18-20; John 4:10; Acts 2:38, 10:45; Romans 6:23; 1 Corinthians 7:7, 13:2; Ephesians 2:8; James 1:17; 1 Peter 4:10)

"For as Jonah was three days and three nights in the belly of the great fish, so will the Son of Man be <u>three days and three nights in the heart of the earth</u>. The men of Nineveh will rise up in the judgment with this generation and condemn it, because they repented at the preaching of Jonah; and indeed a greater than Jonah is here. The queen of the South will rise up in the judgment with this generation and condemn it, for she came from the ends of the earth to hear the wisdom of Solomon; and indeed a greater than Solomon is here."
– Matthew 12:40-42

Abraham, Samuel, David and the souls of all other believers who died before Jesus died on the cross were being held captive in Paradise, waiting until Jesus retroactively died on the cross for their sins so He could then come down to Paradise to rescue them and take their souls and spirits back with Him and up to Heaven (Hebrews 9:26-28)—

"For God presented Jesus as the sacrifice for sin. People are made right with God when they believe that Jesus sacrificed his life, shedding his blood. This sacrifice shows that <u>God was being fair when he held back and did not punish those who sinned in times past, for he was looking ahead and including them in what he would do in this present time</u>. God did this to demonstrate his righteousness, for he himself is fair and just, and he declares sinners to be right in his sight when they believe in Jesus." - Romans 3:23-26 NLT

After the Resurrection of Jesus Christ

Jesus now holds the keys of Death and Hades—

After Jesus was resurrected, He put his right hand on John's shoulder, and said, "Do not be afraid; I AM the First and the Last. I AM He who lives, and was dead, and I AM alive forevermore. Amen. And I have the keys of Hades and of Death." - Revelation 1:17-19.

Since Jesus now holds these keys, the gates of Hades can no longer prevail against believers. But those whose names were blotted from God's Book of Life are still being held in Hades, waiting for their final judgment in the lake of fire. (Matthew 16:18; Revelation 20)

Jesus emptied Paradise when He took believers to Heaven with Him. The souls of believers who currently die now skip Paradise and go directly to heaven to be with the Lord. Paul writes, "So we are always confident, knowing that while we are at home in the body we are absent from the Lord. For we walk by faith, not by sight. We are confident, yes, well pleased rather <u>to be absent from the body and to be present with the Lord</u>." - 2 Corinthians 5:6-8

Paul explains that he is going straight to heaven when he dies: "For to me, to live is Christ, and to die is gain. But if I live on in the flesh, this will mean fruit from my labor; yet what I shall choose I cannot tell. For I am hard-pressed between the two, having a desire <u>to depart and be with Christ</u>, which is far better. Nevertheless <u>to remain in the flesh</u> is more needful for you." - Philippians 1:21-25

Pop Quiz on Hell

Some confusion over what Hell exactly is might be due to some Bibles translating the Hebrew "sheol" as "Hell." But "sheol" can mean pit, grave, death, Hades, Paradise, or may refer to both Hades *and* Paradise as the place of the dead. Sheol, in Jonah's case, was inside a big fish. Some translations simply leave it as "sheol" to avoid bias, which allows us to sort out what each "sheol" means by the context of the passage.

Hades and the lake of fire are real places, but there is actually no third place specifically called "Hell." See if you can determine if it is Hades or the lake of fire that is being referenced in these verses—

Question 1: Jesus said, "But whoever causes one of these little ones who believe in Me to stumble, it would be better for him if a millstone were hung around his neck, and he were thrown into the sea. If your hand causes you to sin, cut it off. It is better for you to enter into life maimed, rather than having two hands, to go to hell, into the fire that shall never be quenched - where 'Their worm does not die, And the fire is not quenched.'" (Mark 9:42-44)

Answer: Jesus is quoting from Isaiah 66:24. This refers to the Lord's future millennial reign that occurs before the last judgment with the lake of fire in Revelation, so Jesus is referring to Hades. Their soul becomes a corrupted sin "worm" in Hades, but does not die.

Question 2: Isaiah wrote of the king of Babylon in Hell—

"Hell from beneath is excited about you, to meet you at your coming; it stirs up the dead for you, all the chief ones of the earth; it has raised up from their thrones all the kings of the nations.

They all shall speak and say to you: 'Have you also become as weak as we? Have you become like us?'

Your pomp is brought down to Sheol, and the sound of your stringed instruments; the maggot is spread under you, and worms cover you." - Isaiah 14:9-11

Answer: These kings are in Hades, also referred to here as Sheol. Souls can see, hear and speak in Hades.

Question 3: Jesus said, "Then the King will turn to those on the left and say, 'Away with you, you cursed ones, into the eternal fire prepared for the devil and his demons. For I was hungry, and you didn't feed me. I was thirsty, and you didn't give me a drink. I was a stranger, and you didn't invite me into your home. I was naked, and you didn't give me clothing. I was sick and in prison, and you didn't visit me.'

Then they will reply, 'Lord, when did we ever see you hungry or thirsty or a stranger or naked or sick or in prison, and not help you?'

And he will answer, 'I tell you the truth, when you refused to help the least of these my brothers and sisters, you were refusing to help me.' And they will go away into <u>eternal punishment</u>, but the righteous will go into eternal life." (Matthew 25:41-46 NLT)

<u>Answer</u>: Jesus describes a future everlasting fire prepared for the devil and his angels, which Revelation 20:15 explains is "the lake of fire," where the souls that are now in Hades will also be punished, which will be their second death. Jesus said, "Do not fear those who kill the body but cannot kill the soul. But rather fear Him who is able to <u>destroy both soul and body in hell</u>" (Matthew 10:28; Revelation 21:8)

<u>Question 4</u>: David said, "I will bless the Lord who has given me counsel; My heart also instructs me in the night seasons. I have set the Lord always before me; Because He is at my right hand I shall not be moved. Therefore my heart is glad, and my glory rejoices; My flesh also will rest in hope. For <u>You will not leave my soul in Sheol, nor will You allow Your Holy One to see corruption</u>." (Psalms 16:7-10)

<u>Answer</u>: Sheol is the place of the dead divided by a deep chasm into Hades and Paradise. David is glad that the physical body of the Lord Jesus will not decompose, and the Lord will not leave David's soul in the Paradise part of Sheol. Acts 2:30-34 and Psalms 49:15 clarifies that Jesus was resurrected with a new spiritual body, and that David was referring to his soul's redemption from Sheol *after* the death of Christ.

<u>Question 5</u>: Christ proclaimed the truth "to the <u>spirits in prison</u>, who formerly were disobedient, when once the Divine longsuffering waited in the days of Noah, while the ark was being prepared." (1 Peter 3:19-20)

<u>Answer</u>: It is Tartarus, the bottomless pit, the Abyss of Hades, the place of darkness where the punished angels are kept who had human offspring in the days of Noah. The inhuman destroying angel Abaddon will be released from Tartarus during the Great Tribulation. Abaddon is also known as Apollyon, which associates him with the Apollon of renowned Greek mythology. Tartarus is also part of Greek mythology. (Genesis 6:4; Proverbs 27:20; Luke 8:31; 2 Thessalonians 2:8; 2 Peter 2:4; Jude 6; Revelation 9:11 DRB, 11:7, 17:8)

Enoch, Moses and Elijah

Enoch, Moses and Elijah are three exceptions to where souls have gone to in the past, and they seem to play a part in Earth's future—

God buried Moses after he died. Satan disputed the body of Moses since he controlled death at the time, and souls were supposed to go to either Paradise or Hades as their bodies decomposed. Michael the archangel, while contending with Satan over the body of Moses, didn't make any reviling accusation, but simply said, "The Lord rebuke you!"

Elijah and Enoch went directly to God without physically dying. Their souls and spirits went to heaven, but the circumstantial evidence also involves their physical bodies—
(Genesis 5:24; Deuteronomy 34:6; 2 Kings 2:11; Jude 9)

Hundreds of years after they left Earth, Elijah and Moses both physically surface six days before Jesus died on the cross. Jesus led Peter, James and John up on a high mountain and they saw Jesus transfigured. His face became as bright as the sun and His clothes radiated with light. Moses and Elijah then appeared with Jesus and they discussed something.

Moses and Elijah might be God's two witnesses during the Great Tribulation. An energy force emanates from their mouths to consume any who try to harm them. They also prevent rainfall, turn the rivers and oceans into blood, and strike plagues on Earth whenever they want. Then Abaddon, the powerful angel beast who emerges from the bottomless Abyss, overcomes and kill them. But no one is allowed to bury them. All the people of Earth gloat, and celebrate their deaths by merrily exchanging gifts. But after three and a half days God's Spirit of life enters them. They stand on their feet and a great voice says, "Come up here!" All the humans of Earth watch aghast in horrified terror as they rise and disappear into a cloud. (Matthew 17:1-4; Revelation 11:3-12)

The souls of believers who now die skip Paradise and go directly to be with the Lord, as Moses evidently did. Believers of the future will physically go to the Lord without dying, as Elijah and Enoch did.

Enoch, who God translated without dying long ago, said, "The Lord is coming with a vast multitude of holy ones to judge the people of Earth and convict them of all the ungodly things they have done, and for all of the ungodly insults they said about God."
(Malachi 4:5-6; Mark 9:2-13; Luke 1:17; John 1:19-23; 1 Corinthians 15:52; 2 Corinthians 5:6-8; 1 Thessalonians 4:16-17; Hebrews 11:5; 1 John 3:2; Jude 14-15)

The Soul Flowchart

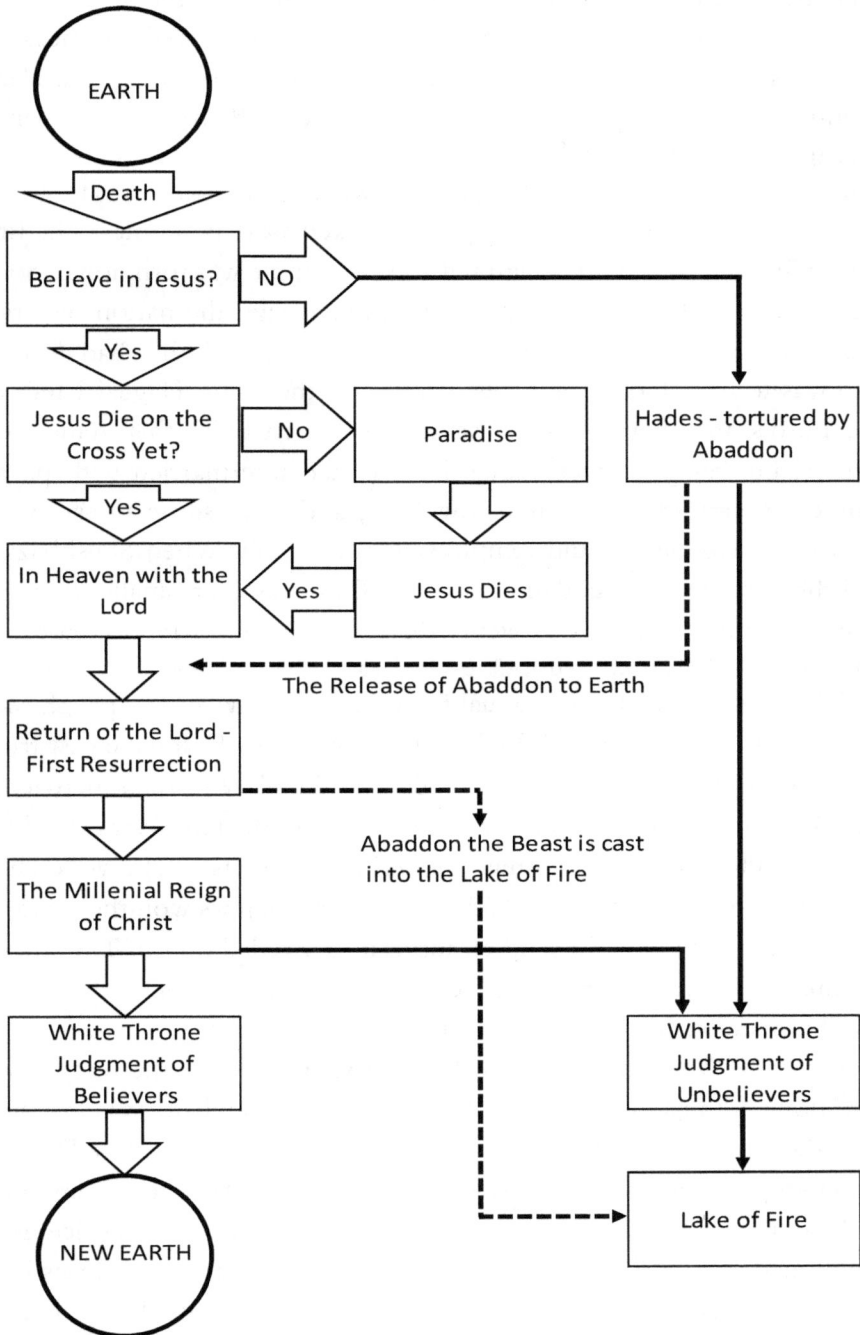

```
        ┌─────────────┐
        │    EARTH     │
        └─────────────┘
              Death

   ┌──────────────────┐
   │ Believe in Jesus?│  NO ─────────────────────┐
   └──────────────────┘                          │
            Yes                                   │
                                                  ▼
   ┌──────────────────┐      ┌──────────┐   ┌──────────────────┐
   │ Jesus Die on the │  No  │ Paradise │   │ Hades - tortured │
   │   Cross Yet?     │ ───► │          │   │   by Abaddon     │
   └──────────────────┘      └──────────┘   └──────────────────┘
            Yes                    │
                                   ▼
   ┌──────────────────┐      ┌──────────┐
   │ In Heaven with   │ ◄Yes │Jesus Dies│
   │   the Lord       │      │          │
   └──────────────────┘      └──────────┘

        The Release of Abaddon to Earth

   ┌──────────────────┐
   │ Return of the    │
   │ Lord - First     │
   │ Resurrection     │
   └──────────────────┘
                          Abaddon the Beast is cast
                          into the Lake of Fire
   ┌──────────────────┐
   │ The Millenial    │
   │ Reign of Christ  │
   └──────────────────┘

   ┌──────────────────┐      ┌──────────────────┐
   │ White Throne     │      │ White Throne     │
   │ Judgment of      │      │ Judgment of      │
   │ Believers        │      │ Unbelievers      │
   └──────────────────┘      └──────────────────┘

        ┌─────────────┐      ┌──────────────────┐
        │ NEW EARTH   │      │  Lake of Fire    │
        └─────────────┘      └──────────────────┘
```

The Eternal Flame

The seven eternal Spirits of God burn before Him in Heaven. God told the Israelites to continually burn a consuming flame as a copy of what is in Heaven, and to use this flame when they offered sacrifices for their sins. The Temple Mount, situated on a hill overlooking Jerusalem, eventually became the place where this continual flame, or daily flame, was always kept burning for these sacrifices.
(Exodus 27:20, 29:42; Leviticus 6:8-13; Hebrews 8:5, 12:29; Revelation 4:5, 15:5)

This continual flame was temporarily taken away two times. The first was in 586 B.C. when Jerusalem fell and the temple was torn down. Soon afterwards, Ezekiel detailed the new temple design the nation of Israel was to use to rebuild it with if they were ashamed of all they had done; it also was to have blood sacrifices offered for their sins. Haggai 1 tells of the Lord's anticipation when the time came to build this grand new temple, but the Jews were not ashamed, had intermarried with pagan women, practiced usury on fellow Jews, and even some priests were defiled, so Ezekiel's grand temple was never built. When Sheshbazzar laid the new temple foundation in 516 B.C., it was even smaller than the first one, and the older Jews wept. (Ezra 3:12, 5:13-16, 9:1-15; Nehemiah 2:10, 5:3-13, 6:14, 13:4-30; Ezekiel 40:4, 43:10-11; Haggai 1, 2:3)

The second time the continual flame was taken away was prophesied of in Daniel 8:10-14 and 11:33-32, when Antiochus Epiphane cast truth to the ground and set up an altar to Zeus in the place of the sanctuary in 167 B.C. The continual flame was cast down and the temple was trodden on for 2300 mornings (Hebrew "boqer") and nights (Hebrew "ereb"). But 1,150 solar days later, in 165 B.C., courageous Jews won their temple back with daring exploits, and cleansed it in a rededication. The Jewish Hanukkah festival observes this rededication, when only one day's supply of oil miraculously burned for eight. (1 and 2 Maccabees)

Only the Western Wailing Wall is left standing after the temple was torn down a third time in 70 A.D. The Temple Mount site was in disuse until the Dome of the Rock shrine was completed in 691 A.D.— Daniel's 11:36-45 prophesy may be referring to this weighty Muslim dominion.

The taking away of the continual (daily) flame of sacrifice isn't mentioned at all in Daniel's 9:24-27 prophesy, but rather that Jesus is to be anointed as the King at the end of the seventieth week, but before this, halfway through that seventieth week, **the blood sacrifice and**

bloodless sin offerings would cease. This was fulfilled by Jesus, who made all blood and daily sacrificing **obsolete** by sacrificing His own life for our sins. Since Jesus permanently ended all blood *and* daily sacrifices, how is God's continual flame represented here on Earth now? (Hebrews 7:23-28, 8:1-13, 9:1-28, 10:18) When the Holy Spirit came on Pentecost, cloven flame-like lights appeared above their heads. Jesus says we are the light of the world, and a light set on a hill cannot be hid— Believers are the temple, light, living sacrifice, priests and kings who now bear witness of God. (Matthew 5:14-16; John 3:19, 5:35-36; Acts 1:8, 2:1-8, 32; Romans 12:1; 1 Corinthians 3:16; Ephesians 5:8; Revelation 1:6, 1:20)

Daniel 12:11-12 prophesies the continual (daily) flame will be taken away for 1,290 "yohms", and blessed are those who wait for 1,335 "yohms". "Yohms" can mean a time of "days" or "years". This prophesy is now unclear, but it may correlate to God's two lampstands burning His flame before Him in heaven, who become God's two witnesses on Earth for the 1,260 days during the tribulation as the saints are overcome by the beast angel Abaddon, who also overcomes these two witnesses. (Zechariah 4:11-14; Revelation 11:3-5, 13:7-8, 18:24)

In the very end, there will no longer be any temple at all in God's new city, because God the Father and Jesus will dwell with us and be the temple, and Jesus will be the light. (Revelation 21:22-23, 22:5)

The Antichrist

The Greek "antichristos" is mentioned *only* in 1 John 2:18,22, 4:3, and 2 John 7. John explains the antichrist that they heard was coming and is already here are those who deny the Father and the Son and don't confess that Jesus came in the flesh. The angel beast and the false prophet of the tribulation *are* antichrist, *but* the Greek "antichristos" is never actually mentioned or used at all in Revelation! (Daniel 7:11; Revelation 19:20)

The passages about Antiochus Epiphane (Daniel 8:23-26 and 11:30-35) likely serves as an analogy of the false prophet of Revelation 13:11-18, but Daniel 8 and 11 prophesied of Alexander the Great and how his kingdom was to be broken into four smaller kingdoms, and of the events after Alexander— These later events depict many different nations and kings encompassing hundreds of years, and are symbolized as the king of the North and the king of the South. (According to legend, Jewish leaders deterred an invasion by greeting Alexander and showing him the passages in Daniel that prophesied of his greatness and coming to them.)

Heaven's Angels

Do angels dwell on Earth, or in Heaven, or somewhere in between? Where exactly *is* Heaven? There are actually three different heavens:

1) The first heaven is our atmosphere. (Acts 14:17; Deuteronomy 28:12)

2) The second heaven is the work of God's fingers, the God ordained Universe of planets, stars, constellations and galaxies. Earth is God's footstool and the Universe is His throne, His house. God has many dwelling places among the stars, but God the Father doesn't dwell on Earth or in the far reaches of the Universe. (Deuteronomy 4:19; 1 Kings 8:27; Psalms 8:3; Isaiah 13:10, 66:1; John 14:2; Acts 7:49; I Corinthians 15:40)

3) God the Father dwells in a third heaven beyond the Universe in timeless eternity. The Ancient of Days, the high and lofty Holy One, said, "I live in the high and holy place but also with those whose spirits are contrite and humble, and where there is an assembly in the far reaches of the north." God's Son interacted directly with humanity and Satan throughout the Old Testament. Born as Jesus, he was made a little lower than the angels, killed and resurrected, and ascended to the third heaven for *us*, and sat down at the right hand of God the Father, at the throne of the Majesty. Stephen, just before his martyred death, saw Jesus standing in the third heaven next to God the Father.
(Job 1:6-12; Daniel 7:9,13,22; Isaiah 14:13,57:15; Acts 7:55; 2 Corinthians 12:2; Ephesians 4:10; Hebrews 2:7, 8:1, 9:24)

The angels of children beholding the face of God the Father are in this third heaven, a hundred million angels surrounding God's throne. (Psalms 113:4-6; Daniel 7:10; Matthew 18:10; Colossians 2:18; Revelation 7:11)

Some of heaven's angels come to Earth. Angels are spirits, and can also have visible, physical and powerful superhuman embodiment. They can blind humans, cause mass deaths, and shine like lightning. It was an angel who stirred the Pool of Bethesda and healed the first human to step into the water. Some believers have unknowingly invited strangers, who were actually angels, to eat and stay in their home. Jesus will send His angels to gather His elect from one end of heaven to the other. Jesus will come back to Earth with His angels. Angels have their own languages. Believers can be a good or bad examples for the angels. The Devil has his own angels as well. Humans are a little below the angels.
(Genesis 19:11, 28:12; 2 Kings 6:17, 19:35; 1 Chronicles 21:15; Psalms 104:4; Daniel 9; Matthew 16:27, 24:31, 25:41, 28:3; Luke 1:19; John 1:51, 5:1-4; I Corinthians 11:10, 31:1; Hebrews 1:13-14, 2:7-9, 13:2)

Stars – Celestial Bodied Beings

Stars are symbols of power, like a scepter. Jesus is the bright morning star. Angels are also stars, like the seven stars which are the seven angels of the seven churches, or the stars from heaven who fought for Israel. God walks on the vault of the lofty stars of the Universe and established ordinances among the stars, and **set their dominion over Earth**, but God can seal up these stars. Some stars do not dwell in eternity with God. (Genesis 37:9, Exodus 32:13; Numbers 24:17; Deuteronomy 1:10; Judges 5:20; Job 9:7, 22:12-14, 38:32,7; I Corinthians 15:38-40; Revelation 1:16-20, 2:28, 8:13, 12:1, 22:16)

The Lord can bring down those who reside in the stars— Lucifer, the day star and son of the dawn, fell to Earth. Also, some angels did not keep their first estate; they left their own habitation and shamefully wandered to Earth and sinned. These wandering stars are now locked in utter darkness. Israel may have worshipped some of these wandering angels, such as Moloch and Rephan. Will the dangerous wayward celestial bodied beings who are cast to Earth and have open human contact during the Great Tribulation be worshiped? Will they present themselves as evolutionarily advanced extraterrestrials? If so, will some falter in their faith?— (Genesis 6:4; Isaiah 14:12-13; Matthew 25:31; Acts 7:42-43; Jude 1:6-13)

When Michael and his angels cast Satan and his angels down to Earth, Satan sweeps one third of the stars along with him. There is no place found in the Universe for them, and they fall spectacularly to Earth like a fig tree casting its unripe figs when it is shaken by a strong wind. Those who dwell in the stars rejoice when Satan and his stars (Satan's angels) are cast to Earth, but those living on Earth are warned of the woes to come— Wormwood, a great star, comes blazing through our atmosphere like a radioactive torch-lit spaceship and toxically pollutes a third of Earth's water, causing many deaths. Then, a fallen star is given the key to the shaft of the abyss, which could be deep within the Earth, or deep in space, or in another dimension, but it has a shaft leading to Earth. The portal to this abyss is opened and Abaddon, the angel king of the Abyss, a dangerous highly-intelligent beast, emerges from the dense, black smoke with his army of weaponized creatures, and they torment humanity. Then, four angels and their formidable flying army of two-hundred million flying extraterrestrial crafts are released. (Isaiah 34:4; Daniel 8:10; Amos 5:8; Obadiah 4; Mark 13:25; Revelation 1:18, 6:13, 8:10, 9:1-19, 12:4-13, 17:8)

ATDs - Angelic Transportation Devices

In the 60 Minutes broadcast, "Navy pilots describe encounters with UFOs", Luis Elizondo and Christopher Mellon explain how they quit their high-level government jobs to help get UFO evidence before Congress and to the general public. Evidence such as jet pilot lieutenant Ryan Graves saying UFOs were observed every day by jet pilots for more than two years off of the coast of Virginia. These disclosures led to the Pentagon releasing a report on UFOs in June, 2021. Humanity has nothing close to this vastly superior technology—UFOs have been clocked flying 43,200 mph, executing instantaneous acceleration and deceleration with calculated G forces of 600, and can travel over 3,315 mph underwater in our oceans! By comparison, a nuclear submarine is limited to about 30 mph underwater, because water compresses very hard like concrete at higher speeds.

"Estimating Flight Characteristics of Anomalous Unidentified Aerial Vehicles" by Knuth, Powell, and Reali; *USOs? Unidentified Submerged (?!) Objects* (Chris Lehto – YouTube)

The Bible doesn't explain how all angels transport themselves. Some angels fly with wings and wheels, such as the six-winged seraphim and two or four-winged cherubim who dwell with God in timeless eternity, but there is no mention of the other angels with humanlike forms having wings, contrary to many old paintings, but these angels are somehow able to fly, but it never explains how. They do need transportation to get to and from Earth, such as the angels using a ladder in Jacob's dream. The angel Gabriel said he was *caused* to fly swiftly to Daniel at the beginning of Daniel's prayer, and got there at the end of Daniel's prayer, so it took Gabriel about 3.5 minutes to physically travel to Daniel. What caused Gabriel to fly so swiftly? Could it be that some UFOs are fantastic angelic transportation crafts so technologically advanced that they antiquate the spacecraft of *Star Wars* and *Star Trek*? It's unlikely angels are using 5,000-year-old human chariot technology! It is likely angels have much better technology than humans. (Zechariah 1:20; I Corinthians 15:40; Hebrews 2:7)

If UFOs do transport angels, are they good or bad angels? Could it be that there are 21 different types of angelic species, 14 of whom are aligned under God's angel Michael, and 7 types of heavenly species, or a third of them, who are ruled by Satan? (Revelation 12:3-12)

The Hebrew word "soos" means "skipping like horses and darting about like swallows" and is often translated as "horses", but in some cases it is used to describe some curious flying devices, such as the ones described in Zechariah called "the four spirits of heaven" who patrol Earth. The Lord's host of glowing fiery orange-red transportation devices protecting Elisha from a hostile human army were described as skipping and darting. The glowing, fiery orange-red transportation device that flew in and separated Elijah from Elisha was also described as skipping and darting, just before Elijah was taken away in a whirlwind-like vortex force. Elisha called this flying device, "the chariot of Israel and its chariot drivers", indicating that he had also seen pilots in this device. (2 Kings 2:12, 6:17) Is it just an interesting coincidence that the 1947 appearance of UFOs near Roswell, New Mexico coincided with Israel becoming a nation again? Are some UFOs the protecting "chariots and chariot drivers of Israel" from long ago that have now reappeared? Their planet-wide behavior around nuclear power and weaponry supports this speculation. Details of their behavior are documented in the evidence-driven books *UFOs and Nukes* by Hastings, *In Plain Sight* by Coulthart, and *UFOs: Generals, Pilots, and Government Officials Go on the Record* by Kean.

Zechariah 1 states: In a vision at night I saw a man piloting a red transportation device that was skipping and darting over by myrtle trees that were at the bottom. Behind him were other red, bright startling red, and white transportation devices that were skipping and darting about.

I asked, "What are these, my lord?!"

The angel said, "I will show you what these are."

The man over by the myrtle trees said, "These are they who the Lord has sent to patrol Earth."

They answered the Angel of the Lord by the myrtle trees, "We journeyed all over Earth, and have found that it is at peace and resting."

Zechariah 6 states: I looked up and saw four transportation devices coming out from between two mountains. The mountains were made entirely of brass.. The first transportation device skipping and darting about was red, the second transportation device skipping and darting about was black, the third transportation device skipping and darting about was white, the fourth transportation device skipping and darting about was grizzled like hail, and tan.

I asked the angel, "What are these, my lord?"

The angel said to me, "These four spirits of the air and outer space have come from the presence of the Lord of Earth who rules this place at this time. The black skipping and darting objects will go North, the white go toward after them, and the grizzled like hail will go South.

The tan came out from them and begged and beseeched and sought to go and depart and vanish to patrol Earth.

The Lord said, "Go, depart and vanish to patrol Earth."

So they departed and vanished to patrol Earth.

A literal translation of Habakkuk 3:8 and 3:15 says of the Lord's "chariot", "You pilot your skipping and darting transportation device of aid and deliverance. You push through the sea with your skipping and darting transportation device, pushing the water aside like clay cement."

Was the Lord in His misty and fiery-lit cylindrical ATD of salvation while escorting the Israelites out of Egypt, when the Lord looked down and saw the pursuing Egyptian chariots riding between the standing walls of the Red Sea, or when David later saw Him suspended in midair? Did the Angel of the Lord fly over the tops of the mulberry trees into battle before David in an ATD? David wrote that there are 20,000 ATDs piloted by thousands of angels, and the Lord is among them! (Exodus 14:24; 2 Samuel 5:24, I Chronicles 21:16; Psalms 68:17, Joel 2:1-11; Habakkuk 3:8)

Some ATDs may be piloted by wayward angels— The Bible explains the heavens are now in a great spiritual conflict. God created the thrones, dominions, principalities, and the powers who dwell there, and they are not currently visible to us, but we are visible to them, and believers are even on display as in a theatre to them. There is a great war waging among these angels, those who reside in space. Some of these celestial angels are on God's side and travel to Earth to help humans. Some angels are on Satan's side and travel to Earth to preach a false gospel. Some angels have been locked up for misbehavior. (Daniel 7:27; Acts 10:22, 12:7, 27:23; I Corinthians 4:9; Galatians 1:8-9; Ephesians 6:12; Colossians 1:16; Hebrews 1:14; 1 Peter 1:12, 3:22; 2 Peter 2:4, 2:11; Jude 6; Revelation 5:5-13, 12:7, 22:8-9)

Some people claiming contact with extraterrestrials relate that these "higher life forms" encouraged them to telepathically meditate and reach out to them for help in bringing peace and technology to humanity.

1 John 4 states we should not believe every spirit, but test the spirits to see if they are of God, by knowing if they confess that Jesus Christ is the Son of God who came in the flesh. If those on or under the earth, or in heaven or the sea, claim that Jesus was from them, or was just a very important teacher, then they are not of God. (Philippians 2:5-11)

The Angel Beast from the Abyss - Abaddon, a.k.a. Apollyon

Long ago God had the angel Abaddon locked into the Abyss, also known as the Bottomless Pit. The Hebrew "Abaddon" is usually translated as "destruction" in the five verses which give the terrible context for what Abaddon does in the place of the dead to those who rejected the Lord—

All that Abaddon does is fully exposed and open before the eyes of the Lord. Abaddon is as an unquenched fire that is never satisfied with having done enough. He burns everything of value in those dead souls who are doomed for destruction by using their iniquity that is deserving of judgment as a fire to consume their souls down to the very roots of everything that they have of value so that all that remains of their souls is an undying, withering worm. Just as our eyes are never satisfied, so Abaddon is never full or satisfied with all of his consuming of lost human souls who did not believe in the Lord. God's love and faithfulness is not declared in this place of the dead, where Abaddon is. Death and Abaddon say, "We have heard a rumor with our ears of Wisdom and Understanding." But the Lord knows the way to Wisdom, and the Lord knows the place of Understanding. (Job 26:6, 28:22, 31:12; Psalm 88:11; Proverbs 15:11; Proverbs 27:20; Isaiah 66:24; Mark 9:47-49)

When this destroying angel is released from the Abyss with a key, then Abaddon, also known as Apollyon and later referred to as the Beast from the Abyss, leads an invasion of loud flying insect-like creatures with golden headgear, humanoid faces, long hair and vampire teeth who inflict terrible pain with their scorpion-like tail stingers for five months. After being cast from the heavens, Satan and his angels help Abaddon rise to power. After Abaddon's head is mortally wounded and he miraculously heals, humanity marvels and says, "Who is like him, and who is able to make war with him?" They worship Abaddon, and Satan. Abaddon is highly-intelligent with amazing speaking abilities, and blasphemes God and those who dwell in heaven. He wages a war and overcomes believers in Christ. He gains authority in every nation and place on Earth, and his false prophet then has believers killed. Everyone whose names aren't written in the Book of Life will worship him. God warns us when this happens that those who lead others into captivity will go into captivity, and those who fight back and kill others will also be killed. God advises us to just be patient in our faith. (Luke 10:17-20; Revelation 1:18, 9:1-11, 12:7-13, 13:1-18)

A New World Order - Deadly Superheroes

After Abaddon is released from the Abyss, God allows four angels to be unbound. They command two-hundred million riders, who kill a third of humanity. These riders have superhero-colored fiery red, hyacinth blue and sulfur yellow body armor. This is about one rider for every thirty-five humans. They ride in flying armored devices with powerful fronts which expel deadly sulfur dioxide gas and molten sulfur, and they have cunning, malicious tails. Near the end, Abaddon also enlists the assistance of Earth's ten new kings to demolish Earth's cities, global marketing and financial systems. About five billion humans die during this terrible time—from Satan's war on believers and humans, and from God's judgments. (Daniel 7:25-27; Revelation 6, 9:1-21, 13:1-18, 17:8,15-18)

The False Prophet

A second beast emerges from the earth, an insidiously fascinating false prophet of deceitful words and miracles, who amazes the world by calling down fire from heaven. He gains control over Earth's computers and systems. After Abaddon miraculously survives his head wound, this false prophet has humans make an image to Abaddon, and then gives this image an artificial intelligence and life, or a soul, so it speaks. This artificial lifeform might arise from genetically altering injections, and/or artificial intelligent software that infiltrates humanities' smart phones and electronic devices to track down and kill all those who won't worship this image of Abaddon. Only those who have Abaddon's mark, name or number on their right hand or forehead can buy or sell. Believers are then slaughtered in a global Christian genocide, and their deaths are physically avenged with the six bowls of God's wrath.
(2 Thessalonians 2:1-11, Revelation 13:11-15)

The Mark

Those who get the mark **and** worship the beast will be cast into the lake of fire. This "**and**", translated from the Greek "kai", means "**both**" or "**also**". "Kai" is used in all four passages about those who worship the beast **and also** get the mark. (Revelation 13:16, 14:9-12, 16:2, 19:20, 20:4)

What happens to those believers who get the mark of the beast, but don't worship the beast? Will they lose their hope, their guarantee of an eternal life? Or, like Peter, will their receiving this mark be considered a denial of Jesus, something the Lord can use for His good in drawing them closer to Him? Could it be that some believers who get the mark to buy and sell will be like Shadrach, Meshach and Abednego, in that they participated in King Nebuchadnezzar's system of government, but refused to worship this king as a god? For those believers who do get this mark, will this deed be counted as wood, hay and stubble, and not a work of lasting value for eternity? Revelation 15:2 states that those who had victory over the beast **and** the image of his mark **and** the number of his name will stand on the sea of glass with harps of God.

Revelation 13:17-18 says wisdom is needed to understand and calculate the number of the name of this beast; it is the number of a man, 666. The Hebrew spelling of Caesar Nero adds up to 666, so this Roman emperor's 64 A.D. brutality against believers may serve as an analogy of how Abaddon and his false prophet will wage their war against believers. (Hebrew letters also stand for numbers. For example, the Hebrew "6" is the sixth Hebrew letter "Vav", which was original written as a "W" in the Hebrew. So, "666" is the old Hebrew "WWW".)

First Four Seals and the Lord's Four Spirit Horses, and the Trumpets

Zechariah provides the backstory for the four horses of Revelation 6. In Zechariah 1, the riders of the red, white, and brown horses (or rather angelic pilots if these "horses" are angelic transportation devices) are in some myrtle trees after returning from a patrol of Earth. The riders tell the angel of the Lord that Earth is resting peacefully. In Zachariah 6 these horses, and a black horse, are sent out for the Lord's work.

The White Horse and crowned rider Goes Forth among the nations and brings victorious conquering— This represents Christ's victory out of Israel over the past few thousand years. Turkey, Germany, England, Spain and the Americas have historically been predominantly Christian. Libya and Algeria were primarily Christian up to the seventh century, before the Muslim religion began to dominate these areas, and some of the other areas as well. (2 Timothy 4:8; 1 John 5:4; Revelation 19:11-12)

The Red Horse is Everywhere and takes peace from Earth and there is war and slaughter— In Zachariah 1 the rider of the red horse is the Lord's angelic messenger who reports back to the Lord of Heaven's armies. In Revelation 6 the red horse takes peace from Earth and there is war and slaughter everywhere.

The Black Horse goes North and there are high food prices— The black horse was not mentioned in Zachariah 1 when Earth was resting peacefully. In Zachariah 6 it goes North to give rest to the Lord's Spirit, where the majority of Earth's food now originates in the vast grain fields of Ukraine and Russia. Revelation 6 reveals the black horse is associated with high food prices. A reduction of grain farming in this land north of Israel will cause worldwide food shortages and high food prices, since chicken and beef are derived in part from these grains also.

The Pale Green Horse goes South and is given authority over 25% of the earth to kill with widespread famine, medical shortages, disease, and wild beast(s)— The brown horse patrolling the peaceful earth for the Lord in Zechariah 1 becomes grizzled and bay horses in Zechariah 6, and the bay horse is eager to patrol Earth again and is sent out. The Hebrew for "grizzled" means spotted, as if spotted by hail. This corresponds to the fire and hail, which may be meteorites, that cause a third of Earth's trees and grass to burn after the first trumpet of Revelation 8:7. It becomes a pale green horse in Revelation 6, which may represent this wilting and burning of the green grass and trees. If one third of Earth is hit by the meteorite blast south of Israel, then Africa, Brazil, and fringes of Europe and the eastern part of the United States will be affected. It's unclear if the brown horse is changing to grizzled and bay and then pale green, or if they are all separate horses.

The rider's name of this pale green horse is "Death", and "Hades", the place of condemned souls, follows after him. This associates the rider of the pale green horse with Abaddon, the destroying angel beast from Hades. There is a killing "beast" that is also with this pale green horse, it is translated from the Greek "therion" and used later in Revelation 17:8 for the "beast" from the Abyss, which is the angel Abaddon—

In Revelation 9:1-2, a star falls to the Earth from space and is given the key to the shaft of the Abyss. This star then releases the angel Abaddon, who is the beast (therion), from the Abyss of Hades. This indicates that Death, the rider of this pale green horse, may play a part in giving the key for the shaft of the Abyss to this star (stars are angelic off-planet beings who are not from Earth). Abaddon may emerge from this portal abyss in Africa, since the pale green horse goes south and is given authority there over one fourth of the earth. (Revelation 1:18, 20:14)

The fifth seal of martyred saints and the sixth seal with the great earthquake in Revelation 6:9-17 occurs after the beast and the false prophet are on earth. (Revelation 12:17, 13:15, 16:18, 20:4)

Overlapping Revelation Events in Chronological Order

1st SEAL White Horse - Babylon the Great	2nd SEAL Red Horse - Peace is taken from Earth	3rd SEAL Black Horse - Scarcity of food	4th SEAL Pale Green Horse - Death with Hades	5th SEAL - Martyrdom Deaths and the 2 Witnesses / 6th SEAL - Earthquake	Events
					War in Heaven: Michael v. Satan Rev 12:7-12
					The 7 Trumpets Rev 8
					1. Meteorites - 1/3 of land burns
					2. Mount of Fire - 1/3 of sea burns
					3. Wormwood - 1/3 of fresh water is polluted
					4. Earth's Sky is Blocked - 1/3 of sky is blocked
				5th SEAL - Martyrdom Deaths and the 2 Witnesses	5. Abaddon and Locusts - Abyss opens Rev 9
					6. 4 Angels unbound and 200 million pilots
					Abaddon the Beast begins his rule of Earth
					The False Prophet's Miracles Rev 13
					Abaddon's head wound heals
					The Mark - forced worship of the Beast
					*1st Harvest of all Beleivers Rev 14:14-16, 20:4
					7th Trumpet and 7 Bowls of Wrath Rev 11,16
					White Clouds- Jesus approaches Earth Mat 24:30
					The 3 Evil Spirits gather army Rev 16
					The Army of the Beast and the 10 kings Rev 17
				6th SEAL - Earthquake	Earthquake levels the entire planet Rev 16
					The mountains and islands are no more
					Jesus and the saints are revealed in space Rev 19
					Jesus conquers the Army of the Beast
					The Beast and False Prophet cast in Lake of Fire
					Satan is cast into the Abyss

*An angel comes from the temple of God the Father and tells Jesus it is finally the time for the "First Harvest", the "catching away of the saints". (Matthew 24:31-36, I Cor 15:52, Revelation 14:14-16, 16:15)

Subsequent Events after the 7 Trumpets and 7 Bowls of Wrath

Millenial reign with Jesus for 1000 years Rev 20

Satan is then released from the Abyss and rebels with the nations

Satan is cast into the Lake of Fire

Old Earth burns with fire

White Throne Judgment

1. The 2nd Harvest of unbeleivers - Second Death Rev 14:17-20

2. The deeds of beleivers are judged and rewarded I Corinthians 3:11-15

Death and Hades are cast into the Lake of Fire

New Earth - All things are made new Rev 21

New Jerusalem - God's City decends

God's Throne, River, Street, and the Fruit Tree of Life Rev 22

The Rise

Is there to be a rapture in which Christians still alive on Earth suddenly vanish and leave behind a pile of clothes before a great tribulation? Many fictional books on eschatology, which is the study of biblical end times, have portrayed a vanishing rapture *before* the great tribulation, such as *In the Twinkling of an Eye*, published in 1911. The origin of this belief, of Christians suddenly disappearing before a seven-year tribulation, is attributed to John Darby back in the 1800's. The 1909 *Scofield Reference Bible* helped popularized this idea of a rapture, which became a strong belief for many since then. Clarence Larkin, whose charts from his 1918 book *Dispensational Truth* influenced conservative churches, reinforced this as a doctrine. *The Late Great Planet Earth*, published in 1973, proclaimed this rapture would occur before 1990. Then came the *Left Behind* series of the 1990's. These books have been instrumental in leading many to believe in Jesus, which is a good thing. The problem is, this idea of a rapture before the tribulation is based on an opinion, or an interpretation, of a few verses, and could very well be in error. Could there be a rapture before the tribulation? I've thought so in the past. I read *In the Twinkling of an Eye* in my teens, had a *Scofield Reference Bible*, was raised in a conservative Christian group that used some charts from *Dispensational Truth*, read *The Late Great Planet Earth*, and watched a movie adapted from *Left Behind*.

This idea of a "rapture" is based in part on 1 Corinthians 15:52, which reveals that the bodies of mortal believers will put on immortality in the "twinkling of an eye" at the "last trump". While I was investigating the relevant passages and the book of Revelation, it slowly dawned on me that I had unfortunately been wrong about a pre-tribulation "rapture". My investigation found that this physical putting on of immortality in the "twinkling of an eye", when believers are instantaneously transformed into their new physical superbodies, is likely just before Jesus descends down to Earth to wrest it back from Satan. This "last trump" is likely the last seventh trump near the end of the tribulation in Revelation 11:15. I tried very hard, but simply could not prove this twinkling of an eye event occurs *before* the tribulation! ☹

The Day of Christ, when Jesus comes as a thief and we are gathered to Him, is *after* the falling away, and *after* the false prophet is revealed as the man of sin, the son of perdition who exalts himself above all gods. It says to let no one deceive you otherwise. I suspect Christianity will be discredited if a "rapture" does not occur before the tribulation begins, and if so, I hope some believers are not deceived and fall away from or stumble in their faith. (2 Thessalonians 2:1-11)

Jesus said in Matthew 24:36 that even He doesn't know when we will be gathered to Him, and only God the Father knows. Revelation 14:14-16 may tell of when God the Father finally lets Jesus know it is time for this "twinkling of an eye" event— An angel comes from the temple of God the Father and tells one wearing a golden crown who looks like the Son of Man that it is time for Earth's first harvest. Jesus then sends His angels to gather His believers up in a flash, and, as it seems, we are beamed up by their fiery ATDs, just as Elijah was. We are instantaneously transformed into our new quantum-enabled multi-dimensional physical superbodies as we rise to meet the Lord in His great cloud, soon before He descends down to Earth to take it back from Satan. Those who already died, whose souls are already with the Lord, will receive their new superbodies first, then those believers who are still living on Earth will be transformed into theirs also.
(2 Kings 2:11-12; Daniel 7:9-10; Matthew 24:31,42-43; 1 Thessalonians 4:17; Revelation 4:2-5, 6:4, 13:1-17, 19:15)

The Date

Even though Jesus said only God the Father knows when this tribulation will happen and just told us of the signs we should look for, some have still made predictions… Alex Haley, who wrote, *The Late Great Planet Earth*, erroneous predicted a rapture would take place in the 1980's. He based this prediction on Matthew 24:32-34—

Jesus, when privately telling His disciples about the tribulation, said, "This generation will not pass from the scene until these things take place." There has been a longstanding speculation that this generation began when Israel became a nation in 1949. However, if this idea is true, which it could be, the Bible doesn't spell out exactly how long this generation is. For example, God says in Genesis 6:3 a lifespan is 120 years, Psalm 90:10 indicates 70 or 80 years. Genesis 15:16 says that the Israelites would be in Egypt for 4 generations, or 400 years, but they were actually there for 10 generations, which is 40 years per generation. So, is a generation 40, 70, 80, 100, or 120 years? It's unclear. Alex Haley figured a generation was 40 years and thought the rapture had to be before 1990.

The Millennial Day Theory

The Millennial Day Theory speculates that the seven days of Genesis represent a 7,000-year time period for modern humanity. If each "day" of Genesis represents a 1,000-year "millennial day", then the seven days of Genesis may represent seven millennial days. The Millennial Day Theory is based in part on 2 Peter 3:8 and Psalms 90:4, which state one thousand years is like one day for God— The first six millennial days of "work" culminates with the Tribulation, and Christ's millennial reign at the end corresponds to God's seventh day of rest, for a total of 7,000 years.

The first millennial day begins with Adam's exit from the Garden of Eden. The crucifixion of Jesus marks the end of the fourth millennial day, or the end of the first 4,000 years. Counting 2,000 years from His crucifixion places the end of our 6,000-year period at *about* 2033 A.D. (Our current calendar system counts the years from His *birth* until the return of Jesus, but if we instead counted the years from His *crucifixion*, then our current year 2033 A.D. would actually be *about* the year 2000)

This theory indicates the 6,000 years will end in 2033 A.D. However, the exact year of Christ's crucifixion has not been pinpointed, and, since the Lord has said it is not for us to know when this great tribulation will occur, then any speculated future date is doomed for failure. (Acts 1:7)

If there is *some* truth to this speculation, then the end of our modern humanity may end soon with the R-rated extraterrestrial events of the tribulation which seems to coincide with Satan and his angels being cast down to Earth— Abaddon emerges from a portal with abominable creatures who torture humanity for 5 months, two-hundred million extraterrestrials invade earth, two thirds of humanity are killed off, two witnesses from the Lord kill anyone who attacks them, the killing off of anyone who won't worship Abaddon, the global economy and structures are destroyed, the six bowls of God's wrath (similar to the Egyptian plagues with Moses), the sign of Jesus coming from deep space, the gathering of a great army to fight Jesus and His army now visible in a great cloud, God's huge earthquake levels the mountains and islands, and Abaddon's great army fight God and are quickly vaporized.

Regardless of if this theory is true, the amazing 1,000-year reign of Jesus Christ will begin soon after the tribulation. Earth will peacefully flourish with long-life spans and great social and technological advancements under the rule of the Lord of the Sabbath. (Matthew 12:8; Revelation 20)

Is the Tribulation 7 or 3.5 Years?

Daniel 9:24-27 indicates how long the tribulation is. The backstory on this passage is that Israel had sinned for a long time, so God allowed the Babylonians to begin trampling on Jerusalem in 606 B.C., when Daniel was taken captive. They later destroyed Jerusalem in 586 B.C., and more Jews were forced to immigrate to Babylon. These Jews yearned for their home country, to rebuild the walls of Jerusalem and their temple, but the Jews were *especially* waiting for their Messiah, who was to become their King and make all things right for them. (Isaiah 11:1-12)

In Daniel 9:24-27, Gabriel reveals to Daniel that, beginning with the command to restore Jerusalem, 490 years are determined to anoint the most Holy, when the Messiah will finally become their King. (Keep in mind a time gap kicked in after Jesus was rejected as their Jewish king and died on the cross, so this prophesy is now suspended and has been put on hold during our current time of the church.) The question is, how much of this 490-year prophesy was used up and how much of it is still left? Knowing how much time is left of this prophesy tells us how long the tribulation will be, because Jesus will become the King at the end of the tribulation. Is the tribulation going to last for 7 or 3.5 years?

Gabriel said first Messiah the **Prince** would come at 69 weeks (each day of a prophetic week is a year, so 69 x 7 = 483 years). Messiah the **Prince** was Jesus who came right at 483 years, and confirmed a covenant with many, but in the middle of this last week of 7 years Jesus was cut off, not for Himself but to end all sacrifices and offerings (Jesus made all sacrificing obsolete per Hebrews 9-10 when He offered Himself as the ultimate sacrifice, God dying for humankind). Gabriel said after Jesus is cut off the tribulation will begin "on the wing of abominations will be one who makes desolate (Revelation 9:1-11), until the consummation is poured out on the desolate (Zechariah 14:12; Revelation 19:21)." Messiah the **Prince** arrived at 483 years, but about 3.5 years later, when He entered Jerusalem to become Messiah the **King**, he was rejected and cut off for the sins of humanity (Isaiah 53:7-8, Daniel 9:26). So, **486.5** years were used up and **3.5** years are still left of this **490-year** prophesy! For the last 3.5 years, the saints will be given into the hand of the beast: Wars, violence, famine and death may precede the beast, but the great tribulation period with its extraterrestrial events seems to be 3.5 years, not 7.
(Daniel 7:25,12:7; John 12:13, 18:37; Revelation 9, 12:14, 19:16)

The Prophesy of Daniel 9:24-27 - in Gabriel's Words

Weeks 70 are determined upon your people and holy city to finish transgression and end sin and make reconciliation for iniquity and bring in everlasting righteousness and seal up vision and prophecy and anoint the Most Holy. From the command to restore and build Jerusalem until Messiah the Prince weeks will be weeks 7 and weeks 62. Again will be built the street and the wall in troublous times.

(The first 49 years *were* troubled times per Ezra and Nehemiah.)

After weeks 62 will be cut off the Messiah but not for Himself.

(When Jesus was cut off **after** week 69 as a sacrifice, the prophesy clock froze.)

The city sanctuary is destroyed. (The temple was destroyed in 70 A.D.)

The flock of the Prince abides until the end comes.

(Jesus is the Prince of Peace per Isaiah 9:5, sits at God's right hand per Hebrews 8:1, and returns as Earth's King per Revelation 19:16. Believers are the flock or people of the Prince of Peace. The beast and the false prophet, the man of sin, are never alluded to as "prince" in the New Testament.)

Flood until the end: War is determined and desolations.

(Deluges of wars until the end, when planet-wide desolations occur)

Last Week - The Two Events Before and After the Cross

For 3.5 Years Before the Cross: Confirms a covenant with many week one. In the middle of the week ceases sacrifices and oblation.

(In the middle of the last week, after His 3.5-year ministry was complete, Jesus confirmed the new covenant at the last supper per Matthew 26:28, and ended sacrifices on the cross per Hebrews 10:12. There is no New or Old Testament context for an evil "covenant". Daniel 11:22 references another prince of the covenant— this was likely Onias the high priest who was ousted by Antiochus Epiphanes.)

After the Cross for 3.5 Years: Against the wings of abominations desolation until the consummation determined is poured on the desolate.

(Abaddon's arrival with winged abominations which inflict desolations per Revelation 9 may re-start the prophesy clock. The bowls of God's wrath, and then the return of Jesus as King, is the consummation "poured" on the desolate at the end of the tribulation.)

Weeks 70 to Make Reconciliation for Iniquity and To Anoint the Most Holy - Daniel 9:24-27

First 7 Weeks (49 years) Begins in 445 B.C. Jerusalem is Rebuilt	Next 62 Weeks (434 prophetic years) To 30 A.D. Waiting until Messiah the Prince	Last Week (7 Years) 70th Week is from 30 A.D. to ?

70th Week - 30 A.D. to Jesus Arriving as King of Earth

First Half of Week 70 - 30 A.D. to 33 A.D.			Last Half of Week 70 - Dates TBD		
Jesus the Prince Arrives after week 69 and the Beginning of week 70	Jesus Confirms the Covenant, is Cut Off, and Ends Sacrifices	Cross Pauses 70 Week Prophesy (This Age)	Abaddon Arrives	Consummation is Poured on the Desolate	Jesus the King Arrives at the End of the 70th Week

Prophesy Pauses - Events From 33 A.D. to an unknown Future Date

The Temple is Destroyed in 70 A.D.
Flock of the Prince Comes - From 33 A.D. until Near The End
Overflowing until The End - War is Determined and Desolations

Daniel's 30 A.D. Prophesy for Jesus

Gabriel told Daniel when Jesus would come as the **Prince**—

"Know and understand that seven weeks plus sixty-two weeks will pass from the time the command is given to rebuild Jerusalem until Messiah the **Prince** comes." (Daniel 9:24-25, Matthew 4:17)

This time span is (7 x 7) + (62 x 7) = 483 years.

This time span begins with the command to rebuild Jerusalem, given by the King Artaxerxes in the first Jewish month of Nisan in 445 B.C. This time span ends with the coming of Jesus as Messiah the **Prince**. (Nehemiah 2:1; Matthew 4:16-17; Mark 1:15; Luke 4:18-19; John 1:36)

> **These prophetic concepts of time need to be understood:**
> Prophetic time is one year for each day.
> Prophetic time is multiplied by seven for punishment.
> The Jewish calendar year is 360 days, with twelve 30-day months.
> (Genesis 4:15,7:11-24,8:3-4; Leviticus 26:18,24,28; Numbers 14:34; Ezekiel 4:6; Revelation 11:2-3, 12:6-14, 13:5)

Beginning with 445 B.C., there were to be 483 prophetic years until Jesus was to come as the Prince. However, this places His coming on the Jewish calendar, not our Gregorian astronomical calendar.

The Gentile (non-Jewish) astronomical year has 365.25 days. Since it has no year zero and skips from 1 B.C. to 1 A.D., time spans that cross over from 1 B.C. to 1 A.D. need to have this "Year Zero" subtracted.

> To convert 483 prophetic Jewish years to our current calendar
> 483 x 360 / 365.25 = 476.06 astronomical years, or 476 years and 21 days from the command to rebuild that was given in 445 B.C.
> Starting at 445 B.C., and subtracting for Year Zero, brings this to 30 A.D. when Jesus began to preach as the **Prince**. The exact year is not historically confirmed, but most estimates are close to 30 A.D.

Jesus had rebuked the Jewish rulers for being a religious "brood of vipers," so they didn't care how many people Jesus had healed, blind made to see, or paralyzed enabled to walk. These self-righteous Jewish religious rulers influenced the Jews to reject Jesus as their **King** about three and a half years later, around 33 A.D.
(Daniel 9:26-27; Zachariah 9:9; Matthew 21:9-11, 27:20; John 12:12-15, 18:37)

Anti-Semitism

The Jews were despised after Jesus was crucified, after saying, "Let His blood be on us and our children." (Matthew 27:25) —

Rome: In 50 A.D. 30,000 Jews were killed, and in 70 A.D. about one million were killed or starved by Titus, who later disclaimed responsibility because it was so horrific. In 135 A.D. Hadrian killed 580,000 Jews, and they were persecuted long after Constantine's Edict of Milan in 313 A.D.

England: In 1096 A.D. all Jews were killed who would not be baptized. In 1190 A.D. Jews were murdered and their homes plundered. English Royalty claimed to own Jews and their possessions, and in 1290 A.D. they were expelled from England.

France: In 1305 A.D. 100,000 Jews were expelled and their possessions confiscated. When they returned, Pastoureaux shepherds drove them away again. In 1683 A.D. Jews were ordered to leave all French Colonies.

Germany: In 1349 A.D. the Black Death hadn't affected Jews as much, due to their clean hygiene standards arising from their Levitical Law. The Flagellants accused them of causing this disease and tried to exterminate them— 2,000 Jews were burned together alive in Strasburg. In 1560 A.D. they were banished from Germany after 3,000 Jewish houses were burned.

Spain: By 1492 the Spanish Inquisition had killed many Jews, and imprisoned others in dungeons. The Iron Maiden was one infamous casket-of-iron torture device; as "her" door closed, rusted blunt knives pierced the shrieking victim's bodies, and they were dropped into a pit below. In 1492 A.D., Ferdinand and Isabella banished all Jews from Spain. Jews came before them and offered a lot of money to revoke this, but the Grand Inquisitor Torquemada came in, holding a crucifix, and accused them of selling out Jesus as Judas Iscariot had. The King and Queen caved under this religious intimidation, and the Jews had nowhere else to go, having already being banned from England, France and Germany.

The tide turned in 1753 A.D. with England's Naturalization Bill, in 1776 A.D. with the Declaration of Independence, and in 1790 A.D. when some Jews were granted full citizenship in France. They had survived as a people without a country, even surviving the Holocaust that had claimed two-thirds of their European population by 1945 A.D. (Zechariah 13:7-9)

Ironically, the persecuted Jews had exposed these barbaric nations to God's superior moral and conduct codes, and civilly influenced them with Old Testament biblical laws, wisdom and proverbs.[18]

Jesus Predestines 1949 A.D. for the Nation of Israel

In Luke 21:24, Jesus said, "Jerusalem will be trampled down by the Gentiles until the time of the Gentiles comes to an end."

It was speculated for centuries that this time refers to a 360-day prophetic year, with each day lasting one year, and, like the 70 weeks of Daniel, were multiplied by seven for punishment. Were the Jews to be without a country for 360 prophetic years x 7 = 2,520 years?

This trampling down began when Daniel and other Jews were first deported from Jerusalem to Babylon in 606 B.C., some 20 years before Jerusalem's destruction in 586 B.C. (Daniel 1:1-7; 2 Kings 24:1; 2 Chronicles 36:5-6; Matthew 1:11; Babylonian astronomical diary VAT 4956)

Converting 2,520 Jewish 360-day years to 365.25 astronomical day years yields 1876 A.D. But Israel did not become a nation then, and this speculation faded away. (360 x 7 = 2,520 x 360/365.25 − 1 − 606 = 1876)

However, since this is the time of the Gentiles, shouldn't a Gentile (non-Jewish) 365.25-day astronomical year be used instead, since both Daniel and Jeremiah switched to Babylonian king accession year dating while under their rule? (The year *after* the king's actual accession was counted as the first by the Babylonians, but as the second by the Jews).

> 365.25 x 7 = 2,556.75 years − Year Zero = 2,555.75 years.
> Counting 2,555.75 years from 606 B.C. ends in 1949 A.D.
> The United Nations officially acknowledged Israel in 1949!
> The US recognized them in 1948, and Great Britain in 1950.

Jesus *does* seem to indicate when Israel would again be a nation per Luke 21:24! Regardless of this interpretation, the prophecies of Jews coming from all lands, no longer as twelve tribes but as a homogenized nation of people in their own country, has certainly come true! (Ezekiel 22:19-22, 20:34, 37:12; Jeremiah 16:14-15)

Hosea 3:4 states when Israel is once again a nation, they "shall abide many days without king or prince, without sacrifice or sacred pillar, without ephod or teraphim"— This perfectly describes Israel in their current state, without a king or a temple or sacrifices.

If the time of the Gentiles ended in 1949 A.D., when will the Great Tribulation begin? Jesus said only God the Father knows this, so any future date set by a human is likely doomed for failure. (Daniel 9:27; Matthew 24:32-36; Revelation 14:15)

The Woman of Israel

God designed us to desire marriage for fulfillment. How a man feels about the woman he loves is how God feels about a nation. The Lord grieves over the loss of relationships with nations of people like a man grieves over a wife he loves who is prostituting herself. (Hosea)

After Israel twisted what is right with fraud and violence, and even sacrificed their own children in fire, the Lord said, "You defiled your beauty on every street corner and offered yourself to everyone in an endless stream of prostitution and promiscuity. They were shocked by your lewd conduct and insatiable lust for new lovers! You have a sick heart to act like such a shameless prostitute. You build your pagan shrines on every street corner and your altars to idols in every square. In fact, you are worse than a prostitute– you're so eager you don't even want to get paid! Prostitutes charge for their services, but you give your lovers gifts to bribe them into having sex with you! So, you are the opposite of other prostitutes, you pay your lovers instead of getting paid! You have played the slut with many lovers; Yet, return to me."

The Church Bride

Christ loves all believers like a husband who greatly loves his wife. Husbands should take care of their wife as if they are caring for themselves. A man who loves his wife is actually loving himself. This is how Christ loves the church. Jesus gave His life for the church, which is composed of all believers, and washed her clean with God's word because He wants her to be without any blemish; holy and faultless. Just as a man is joined to his wife and they become one, so Christ and the church are one. Believers are members of His body, and as in a marriage, are joined to the Lord in one spirit. To the Lord, when believers are immoral, it is like a wife who prostitutes. It grieves Him.

The Prostitute

At the end, during the tribulation, a vast global system rules over all the nations and Earth's masses of humanity. This system is used to buy, sell and ship great quantities of fashionable clothing, jewelry, all kinds of food, merchandise, products and vehicles. The nations love this great global system like a prostitute, and are intoxicated with her wine of passionate immorality. She uses slaves, and buys the souls of humans. Earth's rulers commit adultery with her, because of her desires for extravagant luxury, and Earth's merchants become fantastically wealthy.

She becomes a home for demons and a hideout for foul spirits, and deceives the nations with her sorceries, drugs and pharmaceuticals. She gets drunk with the blood of believers after slaughtering them in a worldwide genocide, and glorifies her evil deeds and cup of terror as she lives on in luxury. She says, "I have no reason to mourn! I am queen on a throne, not like some helpless widow."

But in a single day this vast global system is consumed by fire— Near the end, ten rulers are appointed to ten kingdoms for a brief time. Because God puts a plan into their minds to carry out His purpose and judgment, they unite and give Abaddon their power and authority. These ten rulers and Abaddon hate this prostitute, strip her bare, consume her, and burn what's left. Those who enjoyed her great luxury are terrified by her torment, and mourn as they see the distant smoke rising from her charred remains. They cry out, "All your luxuries and splendor are gone, the luxuries we love so much are gone forever!"

The merchants and shipowners who became wealthy by transporting her great wealth across the oceans weep and mourn because no one is left to buy their goods. The captains, crews and passengers of cargo and cruise ships cry out as they watch her distant smoke ascending, and say, "Where is another as great as this? How terrible! How terrible this is! She was so beautiful, and in a single moment all of her wealth is gone!"

A mighty angel then shouts, "Musicians will never be heard in you again! No craftsmen and no trades will ever be found in you again! The sound of manufacturing will never be heard in you again and your lights will never shine! For your merchants were the greatest in the world, and you deceived the world with your sorceries. In your streets flowed the blood of God's people, and of people slaughtered all over the world."

A vast crowd in heaven then shouts, "Praise the Lord! For our Lord God the Almighty reigns. Salvation and glory and power belong to our God. His judgments are true and just. He judged the great prostitute who corrupted the earth with her immorality for the sake of His believers, and avenged the murder of His servants. Let us be glad and rejoice, and give Him honor because the time has come for the wedding feast of the Lamb, and His bride has prepared herself. She has been given the finest of pure white linen. Blessed are those who are invited to the wedding feast of the Lamb." (Isaiah 62:5; Jeremiah 3:1; Ezekiel 16; 23; Hosea 1-3; John 3:29; 1 Corinthians 6:15-17; Ephesians 5:25-33; Revelation 17:7-19:9)

Immortal Superbodies

Job said, "I know my Redeemer lives. He will stand on Earth in the end after my body has decayed, yet in my body I will see God! I will see Him for myself. Yes, I will see Him with my own eyes!" When they hear of it, some intellectual people make fun of the dead being physically resurrected, but others want to know more—

We are not at home with the Lord as long as our biological shells are alive, but after death our soul and spirit goes to be with the Lord. Will our soul and spirit still be able to see, hear and remember? Samuel's spirit could see, hear, and think when he arose from Paradise to talk with Saul. When Paul was caught up to the third heaven he couldn't tell if he was in or out of his body, but he could still see! In Revelation, when John's spirit entered God's timeless dimension he could still see, hear and recall details about God's throne without the aid of his physical body.

So, why do we even need a physical body? This is the main point that Jesus makes about what He wants to do for us! The Lord told Adam long ago that if he disobeyed, then, "You will surely die." Adam could have biologically lived forever by eating from the tree of life, but after Adam sinned a flaming sword guarded it. So, God foreordained Jesus to provide the way for us to live eternally in new, physically superior bodies.

Jesus said, "**I am the resurrection and the life**: Anyone who believes in me will live, even after they die. Everyone who lives in me and believes in Me will never die." Our soul and spirit lives on. But this isn't enough for God, He wants us to live in upgraded, and vastly superior, new physical bodies, as superior as the sun is to the moon. Paul compared our mortal, aging, disease-prone earthly bodies to a fragile tent that soon perishes, but our new eternal bodies will be an immortal permanent home for our soul and spirit that endures forever.

God wants us to live on forever, not merely with just our spirit, but with amazing new physical bodies! Think superhuman abilities. Amazing ones. Jesus walked through walls, teleported, rose in the air, yet also ate fish and honeycomb after His resurrection. He still looked the same. He still had evidence of his injuries. Jesus showed his disciples that he was not a spirit, but was himself with a flesh and bone physical body. *Everyone* agrees that the body of Jesus was missing after the crucifixion, it was because God had remade His physical body and brought Him back to life!

Believers are now spiritual children of God, and we will someday be physical children of God after He refabricates our new bodies. He will make us equal to the angels who never die, so we won't reproduce. Since our now inferior biological bodies simply can't last forever, no matter what genetic enhancements are made, they *have* to be transformed into immortal ones so we can physically, and eternally, inherit the Kingdom of God. After our bodies are transformed, this Scripture will be fulfilled— "Death is swallowed up in victory. O death, where is your victory? O death, where is your sting?"

Will our bodies be refabricated from our decayed flesh? What of those who were cremated? What of those who decomposed in a corn field long ago, and their atoms later became part of another's body? How will God decide who gets which atom? I suspect ordinary atoms as we know them won't be involved, nor will our decomposed bodies. Just as God didn't explain quantum physics to us, He isn't explaining this mystery either. Perhaps someday He will explain both to us.

Jesus made it simple— Believers will receive new, upgraded physical bodies to live with Him forever on an upgraded and new physical Earth.

We *are* God's children, but God hasn't told us what our new bodies will be like. He just let us know that when Jesus appears, we will be like Him, because we will see Jesus as He actually is. God will give to each one of us the new spiritual body that He wants us to have. Jesus said that this is God's will, and why God sent Jesus, so that all who believe in Him can live forever in new, superhuman bodies that never wear out.

God gave us a hint of the future just after Jesus died— The graves were opened and many bodies of the saints which **slept** arose from their graves, and then they went into the holy city and appeared to many people. This is very interesting, because it explains that those who sleep refers to the physical bodies of those believers who have died.

After Jesus was physically resurrected, his followers watched Jesus rise and depart from their sight into a cloud. As they stood watching this cloud, two men standing nearby in white clothes said, "Why do you stand there looking up at the cloud? Jesus has been taken up, but He will come back to Earth just as you saw Him leave."

Jesus assured us this *will* happen, and said, "You will see me coming in the clouds of heaven."

(See the next section for references)

The Return of the Lord

The descent of Jesus towards planet Earth will be unexpected, but it becomes more obvious that a major event is about to occur after four angels hold back the four (magnetic?) winds of Earth.[19,20,21] Our solar system becomes disturbed and celestial bodies begin falling to Earth. A third of Earth's vegetation burns, a third of Earth's water becomes contaminated, and a third of Earth's sky becomes obstructed.

After this, Jesus will approach Earth with His armies of angels from space in magnificent power on, or in, transportation of some type, but all the people of Earth can see of them are the great clouds that conceal them. They mourn as Jesus and his army approaches Earth in this mysterious cloud. The sight is tremendous. It is obvious a major event is inevitable. With the Lord are the saints and believers who have died.

Jesus said only God the Father knows when this will be. When the unbelievers of Earth are saying, "Everything is so peaceful and secure," then disaster will suddenly fall upon them and they will have no escape. Jesus will unexpectantly raid Satan's earth domain to steal away His believers' physical bodies like a thief in the night. People will be at nightclubs, watching movies or be at weddings, and won't even realize this *global* event is about to happen. Two people will be working in construction or in an office, or two will be in bed, depending on their time zone, and then one will suddenly be taken and the other left.

An angel will come from God's temple to say it is time. Then, with a commanding shout and the voice of an archangel, when the last trumpet is blown God will call His chosen ones. Powerful angels will then gather us up from all over Earth and space—

The physical bodies of believers who "sleep" will rise first from their graves, and each believer's soul and spirit will receive their new, and vastly superior, refabricated body. Job will finally be able to physically stand on Earth and see the Lord with his own flesh and eyes!

The Lord said no one can see His face and live. The Lord covered the face of Moses with His hand as He walked by Moses on Mount Sinai. It may be that we will need these upgraded bodies so that it doesn't kill us when we see the Lord's face (after Moses was in the Lord's *presence*, his face radiated with so much light that it frightened everyone).

After the believers who already died have received their new bodies, *then* the physical bodies of all the believers who are still left alive on Earth will be physically transformed in the blink of an eye, and they too will be caught up into these clouds to meet the Lord. Then, all believers will be with the Lord forever in their new, physical superbodies. But, we will all be up in this great cloud with the Lord, and not yet on Earth.

Satan and his angles have worked through and with Abaddon and his false prophet, utilizing Earth's governments, computers and systems to slaughter millions of believers, and God sends horrible "bowls" of plagues to avenge their deaths. When the sign of Jesus approaching Earth is seen, they send out three unclean spirits, like frogs, to gather and unite the ten kings of Earth and their armies to fight this invader from space— although the Lord actually made them and created Earth.

The clouds roll back to reveal Jesus and His armies, and they descend to fight in Earth's tremendous battle. From the perspective of humans two thousand years ago they are on clean, pure white horses, but from the perspective of science fiction fans they are in gleaming white spaceships. If other white spaceships appear before this on Earth, or rise from the sea, or if anyone performs miracles and claim to be Jesus, it will not be Jesus. Jesus will come from space in a great cloud. After an earthquake levels Earth's mountains and islands, Jesus and His army fly over in perfect formation and the energy force emanating from the front of their ATDs consumes Satan's army so rapidly that their living flesh-their bodies, eyes and tongues, wither away as they stand.

Abaddon and his false prophet are then cast alive into a lake of fire, and Satan is locked away for a thousand years in the same bottomless abyss Abaddon had emerged from. Jesus then begins His millennial kingdom and peacefully reigns on Earth for one thousand years with His believers, and with others who survive this terrible time.

(Exodus 33:23, 34:30; Jeremiah 23:6-8, 25:31-33, 31:32-34; Isaiah 9:6-7; 11; 40; Daniel 7:9-14, 12:1-3; Zechariah 14:6-16; Job 19:25-27; Joel 2:1-11; Matthew 7:23, 24:26-39, 25:12,41, 26:64, 27:52-53; Mark 13:25-27; Luke 20:35-36, 24:39; John 6:40, 11:25-26, 20:20-29; Acts 1:9-11, 17:32; 1 Corinthians 15:35-54; 2 Corinthians 5:1-10, 12:2; Colossians 2:18, 3:4; 1 Thessalonians 1:10, 3:13, 4:13-5:3; 2 Thessalonians 2:8; 1 Timothy 4:16, 6:16; 1 John 3:2; Jude 14; Revelation 1:7, 4:1-6, 7:1; 8; 14:15-20, 17:8, 19:10-20:3)

Those who trust in the Lord will be changed and shall ascend up with wings as eagles. They will tirelessly run and walk (Isaiah 40:31)

The Millennial Reign

As the death of the seed produces a plant, so God will match to each believer's spirit DNA a new spiritual body as different as the sun is from the moon. Our physically weak terrestrial bodies will become powerful new spiritual bodies of majestic splendor, like the resurrected physical body of Jesus, not bound by physics and gravity— When Jesus appears, we will be like Him, because we will see him as He is. We may be able to fly, pass through walls, and teleport.
(Daniel 9:21; Luke 24:31-48; John 12:24; Acts 1:9; 1 Corinthians 15:35-49; I John 3:2)

Believers will have that close personal connection with God and others we so crave at times, but sin prevents us from having. Since we are made in God's image, we will relate to God much more and have a very close personal relationship with Him. We will have already chosen not to rebel against God, but to wholly serve and believe in Him.

The massive earthquake at the end of the Great Tribulation levels Earth's mountains and islands. During Christ's peaceful one-thousand-year millennial reign, the planet may have an incredible interlacing of streams, waterfalls and lakes, with gentle, grass eating lions, leopards, wolves and bears who are all as tame as lambs. Vast, giant forests of Jurassic Era redwood and sequoia trees may again populate much of Earth.
(Isaiah 11:6-9; Haggai 2:6,21-22; Matthew 26:29; Revelation 16:18-20, 20:4-6)

But, at the end of Christ's one-thousand-year reign, Satan is released and once again turns humans against God and His people. Earth is then destroyed by God in the sixth mass destruction event of fire, and from its ashes God will make a new iEarth 7, beautiful beyond imagination.

God will live with us on a new earth with no sea, and wipe every tear from our eyes and love us. No one will ever die or be depressed. There will be no pain. The way we exist now will be gone forever. God will make everything new for His new earth— new laws of physics, new plants, new trees, new animals, new ways of life, new forms of communication, new ways of transporting ourselves, new ways of feeling, new relationships, new wisdom and understanding of God and our environment, new colors, and delicious new satisfying foods. And God Himself will dwell with us in His fabulous new city.
(Isaiah 11:6-9, 65:18-25; Ezekiel 39; Daniel 2:44-45, 3:25; Amos 9:13-15; Zephaniah 3:8-12; Zechariah 8:4, 14:9-16; Matthew 19:28; John 14:2-4; 2 Peter 3:7-10; Revelation 20)

Father's Brilliant City of Light

An angel took John to an exceedingly high elevation above Earth to view our Father's celestial city descending from the cosmos like a beautiful bride. He heard a loud voice from heaven say, "God's dwelling will now be with humans. He will live with them and they will be His people. God will be with us and wipe away every tear from our eyes. No longer will there be death or sorrow or pain, because the old way is gone forever." Then God said, "I now make all things new!"

As John watched from an extremely lofty place, an angel measured this radiantly-golden floating city— It is 1,400 by 1,400 miles square. The 1,400-mile *altitude* of her *gates* places her in Medium Earth Orbit (1,150 miles higher than the International Space Station!).

Her vast 200-foot pure jasper wall rests on twelve tremendous foundational jewels. Twelve angels stand by her amazing twelve open gates. Each gate is made of an enormous dazzling pearl that luminously reflects the incredible lights emanating from this fabulous luminescent city— Her mansions and pavement are made of pure, transparent gold!

Since God *is* her temple, His eternal light fantastically radiates within her transparent gold mansions and pavement, and within her red jasper wall and sparkling jeweled foundation, and brilliantly illuminates Earth below! Earth's dynamic green orb mesmerizingly spins beneath the city's transparent foundation, and vast panoramic celestial views of the Universe are visible above through the crystal-clear red jasper walled-dome of God's interstellar gateway city. The pure Water of Life River streams from God's throne, and in the open square and on either side of the River is the Tree of Life with its healing leaves, bearing twelve fruits.

Revelation says we will no longer need the sun. God is well aware that our sun will eventually burn out. He knew it long before we figured it out, and He has a plan to address it. God will be our light. God put a little info in there at the end to alleviate the concerns of us future humans who learn about astrophysics and worry about the sun burning out someday. It is all going to be okay. This new heaven, earth and city is God's next step in accomplishing what He wants in His manifold wisdom. Jesus is now preparing this city for us in His Father's house with many mansions. God is love. (Psalms 104:5; Ezekiel 47; Matthew 5:5; John 3:16, 14:2-11; 1 John 4:16-19; Revelation 21-22)

Blessed are the meek, for they shall inherit the earth – Jesus

References

1   Fields, Helen. "Dinosaur Shocker." *Smithsonian.com*, Smithsonian
    Institution, 1 May 2006, www.smithsonianmag.com/science-
    nature/dinosaur-shocker-115306469/.

2   Herzing, Denise and Johnson, Christine. *Dolphin Communication and
    Cognition: Past, Present, and Future* (pp 3-13). The MIT Press.
    How Intelligent Are Whales And Dolphins.
    us.whales.org/whales-dolphins/how-intelligent-are-whales-and-dolphins/.

3   Stoeckle, Mark Y., and David S. Thaler. "Why Should Mitochondria Define
    Species?" Human Evolution (Vol. 33 - n. 1-2 (1-30) – 2018). Jones, Andrew.
    Humans and Animals Are (Mostly) the Same Age? June 8, 2018.
    evolutionnews.org/2018/06/humans-and-animals-are-mostly-the-same-age/.
    Sequencing Y Chromosomes Resolves Discrepancy in Time to Common
    Ancestor of Males V. Females. science.sciencemag.org/content/341/6145/562.

4   www.cslewisinstitute.org/CS_Lewis_and_JRR_Tolkien_page2.
    C.S. Lewis and J.R.R. Tolkien – page 2.

5   Galileo and the Inquisition. galileo.rice.edu/bio/narrative_7.html.

6   Stuart, Rhett. *The Bishop Maker.*

7   *Chris Pratt's 9 Rules Acceptance Speech 2018 MTV Movie & TV Awards.*
    www.youtube.com/watch?v=EihqXHqxri0.

8   *Chris Pratt thanks Jesus in first appearance since split at Teen Choice
    Awards.* www.usatoday.com/story/life/entertainthis/2017/08/13/chris-pratt-
    thanks-jesus-christ-first-appearance-since-split-anna-faris/563664001/.

9   Hawking, Stephen. The Beginning of Time.
    www.hawking.org.uk/the-beginning-of-time.html.

10 *God, Design, and Fine-Tuning*, Robert Collins citeseerx.ist.psu.edu/viewdoc/
    download?doi=10.1.1.470.7166&rep=rep1&type=pdf. www.newscientist.com/
    article/mg20227123-000- gravity-mysteries-why-is-gravity-fine-tuned/

11 Rich Deem. *Quotes from Scientists Regarding Design of the Universe.*
    godandscience.org/apologetics/quotes.html.
    Schaefer, Henry. *Scientists and Their Gods.*
    leaderu.com/offices/schaefer/docs/scientists.html

12 NIH Human Microbiome Project defines normal bacterial makeup of the body.
    www.nih.gov/news-events/news-releases/nih-human-microbiome-project-
    defines-normal-bacterial-makeup-body.

13 Key, Alexander. *The Forgotten Door.*

14 Kramarik, Akiane. akiane.com/my-story/.

15 Burpo, Todd. *Heaven is for Real.*

16 *How tech's richest plan to save themselves after the apocalypse*
    www.theguardian.com/technology/2018/jul/23/tech-industry-wealth-futurism-
    transhumanism-singularity.

17 Were the three days and three nights that Jesus was in the grave
    a full 72 hours? bible.org/question/were-three-days-and-three-nights-
    jesus-was-grave-full-72-hours.

18 Durant, Will & Ariel. *The Lessons of History,* "Morals and History".

19 A Flat Earth, and other Nonsense. creation.com/refuting-flat-earth.

20 NASA Spacecraft Discovers new Magnetic Process in Turbulent Space.
    May 9, 2018. www.nasa.gov/feature/goddard/2018/nasa-spacecraft-
    discovers-new-magnetic-process-in-turbulent-space.

21 Magnetic Reconnection in Earth's Magnetosphere. sci.esa.int/cluster/
    51744-magnetic-reconnection-in-earth-s-magnetosphere/.

Websites accessed 11/2019

References

Suggested Reading:
References 1-16.
Also, scripture references given throughout the book are highly recommended.
BOOKS: *Erasing Hell* by Francis Chan & Preston Sprinkle; *Heaven* by Randy Alcorn; *The Case for a Creator / Evidence that Demands a Verdict* by Lee Strobel; *Love Does / Everything Always* by Bob Goff; *Seeking Allah, Finding Jesus* by Nabeel Qureshi; *Mere Christianity* by C.S. Lewis; *The Insanity of God / The Insanity of Obedience* by Nik Ripken; *The Unseen Realm* by Dr. Michael Heiser.

Verse highlights for HEART: HEBREW heart leb (3820) will and intellect: Genesis 6:5, 8:1, 17:17, 42:28, 45:26; Exodus 4:14, 31:6, 35:5-22, 35:26, 36:2, 16:28; Numbers 16:28, 24:13; Deuteronomy 28:65, 29:4; Judges 16:16; 1 Samuel 2:1, 10:9, 27:1; 2 Samuel 6:16, 15:6; 1 Kings 3:12, 4:29, 8:66, 11:3, 18:37, 21:7; 2 Kings 5:26; 1 Chronicles 12:33, 28:9, 29:9; 2 Chronicles 32:26; Psalms 10:17, 12:2, 14:1, 19:14, 33:15, 34:18, 51:10-17, 143:4; Proverbs 1:7, 3:5, 4:23, 18:2, 19:8,21, 20:5, 20:9, 21:4, 22:15,17, 23:19, 28:26, 31:11; Ecclesiastes 1:13-17, 2:15,22, 5:2, 7:3-7, 7:22, 11:10; Song of Songs 8:6; Jeremiah 17:9; Ezekiel 36:26; Daniel 1:8, 10:12; **heart lebab (3824) will, intellect and feelings:** Genesis 20:5, 31:26; Numbers 15:39; Deuteronomy 6:5, 9:4, 11:16, 15:7, 20:3, 28:28,47,67, 29:18; Joshua 2:11, 24:23: 1 Samuel 9:19, 12:24, 13:14, 14:7, 16:7, 17:28, 21:12; 1 Kings 2:4, 8:18,29, 9:4, 10:2, 11:4, 1 Chronicles 29:18; Job 9:4, 34:34; Proverbs 16:23, 25:3; Psalms 4:4, 13:2, 25:17, 28:3, 111:1, 139:23; Isaiah 6:10, 7:2, 10:7, 32:4, 47:8; Zechariah 7:10. **heart mind sekviy (7907)** Job 38:36; **GREEK heart kardia (2588) will, intellect and feelings:** Matthew 5:8, 5:28, 6:21, 11:29, 12:33-34, 13:15, 15:18, 22:37; Mark 2:6, 7:21: Luke 2:19, 6:45, 8:12; 9:47, 16:15, 21:14, 24:25,,32,38; John 14:1, Acts 28:27; Romans 1:24, 5:5, 8:27, 10:9-10, 1 Corinthians 4:5, 14:25, 2 Corinthians 1:22, 2:4, Galatians 4:6, Ephesians 1:18, 3:17, 6:22, Colossians 3:15, Hebrews 3:12, 3:15, 4:12. **sklerokardia (4641) hardness of heart** Matthew 19:8; Mark 10:5, 16:14.

Verse highlights for SPIRIT: Hebrew spirit ruwach (7307): Genesis 1:2, 3:8, 6:17, 8:1, 26:35, 41:8, 45:27; Exodus 6:9, 28:3, 31:3, 35:21,31; Numbers 5:14, 11:17, 11:29, 14:24, 16:22; Joshua 2:11, 3:10, 5:1, 8:3, 9:23; Judges 15:14, 15:19, 1 Samuel 1:15, 16:14, 19:23, 30:12; 2 Samuel 22:11,16; 1 Kings 22:21; 2 Kings 2:9, 2:15; 1 Chronicles 5:26; 2 Chronicles 9:4, 18:20; Ezra 1:5; Nehemiah 9:20; Job 7:11, 10:12, 12:10, 15:13, 17:1, 20:3, 21:4, 32:8,18, 33:4; Psalms 32:2, 33:6, 34:18, 51:10-17, 77:2-6; 78:8, 104:4, 139:7, 142:3; Proverbs 1:23, 11:13, 14:29, 15:4, 15:13, 16:18,19,32, 17:27, 18:14, 29:11; Ecclesiastes 1:14, 4:8, 7:8, 8:8, 11:5; Isaiah 4:4, 11:2, 19:14, 26:9, 29:10, 37:7, 42:1, 48:16, 54:6, 57:15, 61:1,3,10; 66:2, Ezekiel 3:24, 11:19,24, 13:3, 18:31-32, 21:7, 36:26-27, Hosea 5:4; Haggai 1:14; Zechariah 12:1,10, 13:2; Malachi 2:15-16. **Greek spirit pneuma (4151):** Matthew 1:18, 3:15, 4:1, 5:3, 8:16, 10:1,20, 12:18, 26:41; Mark 1:8,27, 2:8, 5:8; Luke 1:15,47, 2:26,27; John 3:5-7, 14:17-26, 16:13, 19:30; Acts 2:38, 5:3,9,16,32; 6:10, 7:55, 8:39, 9:31, 10:44-45; 11:12, 13:2,52, 15:28, 19:21, 20:28, 21:11; Romans 1:4,9, 2:29, 5:5, 7:6, 8:2-27, 12:11, 14:17, 15:30; 1 Corinthians 2:4,13, 3:16, 6:18-20, 7:34,40, 12:3-7, 16:18; 2 Corinthians 1:22, 2:13, 3:3,6,17, 7:13, 11:14; Galatians 3:2, 4:6, 5:16-25, 6:1,8,18; Ephesians 1:17, 2:2, 2:18,22, 3:16, 4:3,22-23,29,5:18; Ephesians 6:17-18: Philippians 1:27, 3:3; Colossians 1:8, 2:5; 1 Thessalonians 1:5-6, 4:8, 5:19,23; 2 Thessalonians 2:2,8,13, 4:1; 2 Timothy 1:7,14; Titus 3:5; Hebrews 1:14, 4:12, 9:14, 12:9, 23:23; James 2:26, 4:5, 1 Peter 1:12, 3:4,18, 4:6; 1 John 4:13; Jude 19-20.

References

Verse highlights for SOUL (LIFE): **Hebrew soul naphash (5315):** Genesis 1:20-24, 30; 2:7, 9:4, 12:5, 12:13, 14:21, 19:17,20, 27:19, 34:3, 35:18, 42:21; Exodus 15:9; Leviticus 17:14, 18:29; Deuteronomy 11:18, 12:20, 13:4,6, 14:26, 18:6, 23:24, 24:15, 28:65; 1 Samuel 18:1, 23:20; 2 Samuel 17:8; 1 Kings 2:4; 2 Kings 2:2,4,6, 4:30; 1 Chronicles 28:9; Job 10:1, 12:10, 18:4, 21:25, 30:25; Psalms 11:5, 16:10, 29:7, 25:7, 25:13, 27:12, 31:7, 34:2, 35:13, 41:4, 42:1-5, 62:5, 94:19, 103:1, 119:20,25,28,81,167, 139:14, 143:8, 146:1; Proverbs 6:16, 11:17, 11:30, 13:35, 14:10, 16:17, 21:23, 22:23-24, 24:14; Song of Songs 1:7, 3:1-4; Isaiah 10:18, 42:1, 57:16, 61:10; Jeremiah 6:8, 38:16. **Greek soul psuche (5590):** Matthew 10:28,39, 11:29, 12:18; Mark 8:26, 12:30; Luke 1:46, 12:20,22; John 10:15; Acts 2:41; 1 Corinthians 15:45, Philippians 1:27; Hebrews 4:12, 10:28,30; James 1:21; 1 Peter 1:9, 2:11, 3:20; 2 Peter 2:14, Revelation 6:9.

Suggested Additional Study: There are online interlinear Bibles that show the original Greek and Hebrew words with Strongs Concordance numbers. These Strongs numbers can be used for Hebrew (Old Testament) and Greek (New Testament) Englishman Concordance (reverse) word searches to see how they are used in context with other verses throughout the Bible.

About the Author— Rhett Otis and his wife live in Virginia and they have four children. He has a Bachelor of Science degree in business management and organizational behavior from California State Polytechnic University, and investigates civil matters and white-collar crimes. Rhett wrote *The Bishop Maker* to help others work through problems buried deep within their subconscious minds by damaging conservative Christian cults. He has believed in Jesus since 1973.

Other Books

God and Humans (matches sound scientific findings to the Bible)

Under the pseudonym Rhett Stuart

The Bishop Maker – When the Battle is for the Subconscious (How to recognized and recover from conservative Christian cults)

Generation Modified (Young Adult science fiction)

God is the God of science, and the Bible is the infallible Word of God, so surely the two have to match. I have found that Genesis matches both our current Era and the last six major Eras, as mainstream geologists and paleontologists understand them. The inconsistences in the first two chapters of Genesis troubled me, and finally making sense of this has increased my faith in God. I've come to realize that God made each of these six Eras, and left behind a little evidence to let us know these prior Eras existed. The truth cannot be found in bending science to match the Bible, or in bending the Bible to match science. The truth is found by calling out to God for understanding, praying, fasting, mediation, and lots of reading and research. The results of this investigation are documented in my book, *God and Humans*. Here are a few excerpts from it—

~~~

Science and the Bible

During a dark time of scientific repression by mainstream Christian orthodoxy[1], astronomer Galileo Galilei published a book in 1632 explaining how our planet actually orbits around the sun. But the ruling church of his time believed that this could not possibly be true, because it was an absolute fact of scripture that the sun rises and goes down.

Didn't the Lord say Himself that the sun rises and goes down? Didn't David say in Psalms that God laid the foundations of the earth so it should not be moved forever? Doesn't the earth have four corners? Galileo threatened their long-held beliefs on something that they could not possibly be wrong about. They convicted Galileo of heliocentric heresy for saying that the earth moves around the sun, which they said, "is false and contrary to the Holy and Divine Scriptures."[2] (Psalms 50:1, 104:5; Malachi 1:11)

Galileo didn't have access to the scientific knowledge we now have to consider if Earth's four corners and four winds refers to the magnetosphere's four-part relationship with Earth's solar wind magnetopause, magnetic reconnection, and the north and south poles.[3,4,5] (Isaiah 11:12; Revelation 7:1, 20:8)

Under the threat of torture and death, Galileo recanted his findings to the ruling religious organization of his place, so they relented and just sentenced Galileo to a lifetime of house arrest.[6]

God and Humans by Rhett Otis

If you could see the earth illuminated when you were in a place as dark as night, it would look to you more splendid than the moon
- Galileo Galilei

Just because opinions are firmly held for a long time, and strongly enforced by powerful people of influence, doesn't make them true.

Some Christians agree that recent scientific findings such as neutral mutation[7] and radioactive testings[8] indicate that modern humans have been around for over one-hundred thousand years.[9] But some Christians argue that it is an absolute fact of scripture that Earth was made in six solar days about six thousand years ago.[10,11,12]

The recent strong push for six solar days of creation might be a reaction to counteract the morally-void theories evolutionists have had taught in public schools, which are now regarded by many as fact. Of how over billions of years dinosaurs evolved from muck, extinct primeval species mutated into new and improved species, and of how, after many new bursts of life, a chimpanzee-type species eventually mutated via natural selection and small random/deterministic drifts of genetic changes into modern humans about 200 thousand years ago.[13,14] These publicly taught evolutionary theories threatened my core beliefs in God, because my belief of six solar days of creation was closely connected to my believing in the Bible's validity, and in Jesus. I was ensnared with discounting sound scientific findings because I thought that they proved evolutionists were right and the Bible wrong. I didn't consciously consider if it was my *understanding* of Genesis that was in error, and that evolutionists were also mistaken about *their* conclusions from this scientific evidence. Could it be that evolutionary theory *and* the proclaimed miracles by six solar day creationists are *both* be wrong?

If God has authored the DNA code during the last 4.7 billion years for all of these new bursts of life, then wouldn't this explain why paleontologists have not found sound evidence for the billions of missing links and intermediary gaps that should exist if these creatures had indeed mutated? Are these links "missing" or "nonexistent"?[17]

What if the first five chapters of Genesis is understood as being literally written verbatim in the same chronological order of time as the events occurred? What if Genesis chapter 1 tells of how modern humans were created on the sixth day about 150 thousand years ago, and Genesis chapter 2 tells of how Adam, agricultural plants and farm animals were made long afterwards, about six thousand years ago?

Sound science generally wasn't considered the bane of Christianity over a hundred years ago. Many respected Christian leaders such as Cyrus Scofield (*Scofield Reference Bible*), Clarence Larkin (*Dispensational Truth*), George Pember (*Earth's Earliest Ages*), Simon Episcopius and Thomas Chalmers thought that there might have been an older Era than ours, and that Earth could be much older than six thousand years.

Georges Culvier, the founding father of paleontology, hotly disputed evolution twenty years before Darwin wrote his book, and Simon Episcopius was preaching of an Era before ours nearly two hundred years before Georges Culvier's first scientific discovery of prior Eras.

Sound scientific findings should *strengthen* a believer's faith.

I do not think it is necessary to believe that the same God who has given us our senses, reason, and intelligence wished us to abandon their use, giving us by some other means the information that we could gain through them
- Galileo Galilei

Would Moses, if he did indeed write most of Genesis and were here with us now, be incredulous that many think Adam and Eve were created on the sixth day, since he plainly wrote that they were made afterwards? He might be irate with whoever twisted his words with this pretentious chapter and verse placement, pointing out that, since the rest of Genesis was written in the same order as the events occurred, then how could anyone possibly assume that the making of Adam and Eve was referring back to and elaborating on the creation of humans on the sixth day?

Did realizing Earth rotates around the Sun disprove the Bible? At some point, religious folk of the past had to stop taking comfort in their complacent religious traditions. Wisdom is realizing when we are ignorant. Worrying about how the truth may negatively impact our relationships with loved ones is not trusting in God. Truth gains honor and value over time. (Proverbs 4:8, 15:33, 30:2; Zephaniah 1:6)

God gave a very simple and accurate depiction of how He created the Universe and planet Earth to an ancient people who were busy obtaining food and water. He understood their perspective, and just told them what they needed to know at that time. Genesis wasn't written as a textbook pre-rebuttal to evolution. The Bible was written for the far more important reason of leading human souls to Christ.

God and Humans by Rhett Otis

Genesis gives a broad overview of our planet's origins to a people who did not know of any Triassic, Jurassic and Cretaceous periods. From their perspective, the sun rose and went down. The most they saw of Earth was as a circle all around them on the horizon while they were high on a mountain top, or out at sea. Just climbing a mountain or going far out into the open sea was dangerous and difficult then.

Scripture is a book about going to Heaven.
It's not a book about how the heavens go
- Galileo Galilei

When sound scientific findings conflict with what we think some passages mean, God wants us to re-evaluate our views, not cling to long-held ideas of limited human wisdom which are simply not supported, or ignore the things which are plainly stated.

It *is* powerful evidence that the Genesis 1 sequence, written long before sound scientific findings, is in a perfect scientific sequence, and that the Big Bang theory at long last essentially proves, or at least supports, that God created the Universe and is stretching it out.

God obviously wants us humans to pursue science. He purposely gave us the abilities and desires to uncover His tantalizing scientific mysteries. He perched Earth in a special place in the Milky Way so that we have a fantastic view of the Universe. He made the sun 400 times larger and 400 times further away from the moon to make possible the unique scientific discoveries that arise from our near-perfect solar eclipses, such as in 1919 when Einstein's theory of general relativity was confirmed. In addition, Earth is in a perfect galaxy to sustain life. It is perfectly positioned safely away from the cosmic explosions near the massive black hole at the Milky Way's center, yet close enough to this black hole to have developed *some* heavy elements, yet safely out of reach of the hazardous Sagittaruis and Perseus spiral arms. (Isaiah 48:13; Job 38:4; Psalms 102:25, 104:5-6)

He stretches out the north upon empty space
and hangs Earth on nothing!
- Job 26:7

The Spherical Earth and Eternal Universe

Galileo understood that the Bible, although still very true, was written to the perspective of those living long ago, and it is also subject to the bias of its translators and expounders. When our spirit detects our biased imprinting might be in error, our soul often reacts in fear by quickly and intensely justifying our errant views. Those who opposed Galileo could not reconcile astrophysics with the Bible. They may have feared risking an empty void of unbelief if they *did* try to understand it.

Although some ancient astronomers thought that the earth rotates around the sun, they also thought the Universe was eternal. They observed the predictable and orderly rotation of the stars across the night sky and concluded from their observations that our Milky Way Galaxy encompasses the entire Universe, and had existed forever. Most scientists agreed with their assessment. However, Christians insisted that the Universe had a beginning, and it began when God created it.

The widely-accepted scientific view that the Universe had existed from eternity was shattered in the 1920's with Edwin Hubble's discovery that some stars are actually rapidly retreating galaxies! It is now widely accepted among scientists that the entire Universe is rapidly expanding, and did not confirm to our currently known laws of physics when the Universe sprang into existence nearly 14 billion years ago.

Historically, humanity has inherently assumed that the Universe revolves around us, and that there are no other creatures of much significance, even though there is ample evidence that we are just a tiny sliver of what God has done in past eons. The Bible's account of modern humanity from Adam to Jesus is just a miniscule part of what God has done in the past, and of what God will do in the future. God just offers us hints, not details, of the distant past, and of the future. The Bible is about God dying in human form to save human souls and spirits, which wasn't done for the angels and the other creatures in the heavenly realm. Perhaps God places so much value on us because we were made in His image. (John 3:16; Romans 8:17; 1 Peter 1:12)

Such is the grasping tendency of the human heart, that it must have a something to lay hold of and which, if wrested away without the substitution of another something in its place, would leave a void and a vacancy as painful to the mind, as hunger is to the natural system
– Thomas Chalmers

Evolution

If God didn't determine our genetic processes, then what force did?

Neo-Darwinistic *and* Modern Synthesis evolution both portray an unintelligent-yet-astonishing deterministic god-like creative force that accounts for our incredible complexity of life. If one were to believe either is a fact, they still don't offer compelling explanations for the evolutionary "bursts of life gaps," or the missing billions of intermediate complex life form links that should exist to support these alleged mystical bursts of mass mutations.

Darwin said, "If it could be demonstrated that any complex organ existed, which could not possibly have been formed by numerous, successive, slight modifications, my theory would absolutely break down."[16] Some modifications do exist,[17] but shouldn't there be ample, *compelling* evidence? Speculating that some creatures *possibly* mutated into other similar-looking ones is a logical idea, but hardly conclusive.

Shouldn't the evidence of these missing billions of intermediary links be obvious and prolific? Evolutionists offer explanations and some possible intermediaries,[19] but concluding they all randomly drifted with small genetic changes into our vast spectrum of living things, both past and present, requires more than just being firmly planted in the soil of scientific self-knowledge. Scientific knowledge itself evolves.

The scientists of *www.thethirdwayofevolution.com* think that Neo-Darwinists have elevated Natural Selection into a unique creative force to solve all of the difficult evolutionary problems without a real empirical basis, and that alternatives to traditional evolutionary theories need to be considered.

A few professionals state on *www.dissentfromdarwin.org*,[18] "We are skeptical of claims for the ability of random mutation and natural selection to account for the complexity of life. Careful examination of the evidence for Darwinian theory should be considered." These professionals hold doctorates from Oxford, Cambridge, Harvard, Dartmouth, Rutgers, University of Chicago, Stanford, and the University of California at Berkeley. Many are also professors or researchers at major universities and research institutions such as Cambridge, Princeton, MIT, UCLA, University of Pennsylvania, University of Georgia, Tulane, and in Moscow, Japan and Israel.

When closely studied, every tiny detail of any living creature is revealed to be an incredible work of art under an electron microscope. Fascinating details emerge about their behavior, symbiotic relationships in how they relate to and help other creatures and plants, their chemical reactions, DNA, unique chromosome strands, molecular engines, and their trillions of cells working together in incomprehensible unity.[20]

Consider the modern medicines that are bioemulated from plants, mold, leeches and tree bark, and the thousands of medicines yet to be discovered. Are they all just miraculous freaks of nature?[20] Consider that one teaspoon of sea water has more living organisms than the entire planet's human population, and a teaspoon of fertile soil has about one billion inhabitants. Consider the billions of neurons forming a virtual living brain in the head and tentacles of an octopus that enable it to change color and sneak out at night to snack on crabs in other aquariums, or the 100k megapixel skin of a cuttlefish, which has a vastly higher resolution than an 8k TV.

Many biologists think that 99 percent of our planet's total species lived during the last five Eras and are now extinct.[22] Have these *billions* of animal species, insects, microbes and plants *really* all been simultaneously, and *very prolifically*, mutating into other species during the last 4.7 billion years?[23] If so, where is the conclusive evidence?

Six billion nucleotide bases make up human chromosomes and are in each of our ten trillion or more cells. Billions of chemical reactions occur each millisecond in every living creature, billions of proteins message, chemically switch off and on, give electrical charges, and this has to all be in near-perfect working order for each creature to just stay alive.[20] The tiniest creature has millions of components working perfectly together in unison, *and* can eat and reproduce. Did this *really* all happen by extremely determined or magical coincidence? Imagine natural forces randomly creating a smart phone chip with only a million circuits, along with the towers and network it needs to function. But a tiny organism is far more complex than a smart phone, and they also require many other life forms to function and exist. All living things depend on the lives of others, and their DNA code is vastly more advanced and intricate than a comparatively simple smart phone that is unable to even reproduce itself.

The DNA Code

What if the DNA of Earth's living creatures all share some universally common evidence of God's authorship? If God did not author our DNA code, then what force did? Dr. Geoffrey Simmons, in his book, *What Darwin didn't know*[20], explains from a fascinating medical viewpoint the improbability of DNA and chromosomes evolving to create the highly intricate genetic code, chemicals, biological systems and emotions of a human—

For example, if the alleged common ancestor of chimpanzees and humans had a brain similar to the size of a modern chimpanzee, about 30 billion neurons, then modern humans would have to mutate a vast <u>60 billion</u> brain neurons in a mere 6 million years to achieve our current 90 billion brain neurons. This assumes humans and chimpanzees had a 6-million-year-old common ancestor.[21] The African elephant brain has 250 billion neurons, making evolution an even more unlikely option.

The consciousness of man, the mind, is something not to be reduced to brain mechanisms - Wilder Penfield, father of modern neurosurgery

Our vast genetic variances and biochemical activities also formidably challenge deterministic genetic drift, requiring an astounding 133 or so predetermined genomic mutation improvements per generation to evolve from a chimpanzee-like creature into the 6-billion-bit human.[20,21]

We have a better chance of winning the lottery every week for the rest of our lives, because it is very rare to evolve even a small *insignificant* spontaneous evolutionary change in 100 years, and also requires *both* DNA lottery-winning parents to have the *same* "defect," and their offspring to be genetically endowed and produce offspring with this same defect, and have that defect be an *extremely* rare spontaneous improvement, and not the *usual* detriment, and that it also continues to be *passed on* to their descendants, so that in a mere 4.7 billion years this magically accounts for all of the vast chemical and molecular complexities of DNA, smell, taste, sight, nerve, muscle and organ functions for our vast millions of living creatures, and also somehow accounts for emotions, humor and art.[20]

We logically assume that there is intelligence behind the design of any computer or machine, so isn't it extremely speculative to argue an unintelligent force created these vastly more complicated creatures?

God and Humans by Rhett Otis

After reviewing and studying the neutral mutations of millions of planet-wide DNA tests from 100,000 different species, two scientists found that 90 percent of our current animal species, including humans, all emerged nearly simultaneously between 100,000 to 200,000 years ago. They also found that our current animal species have a very clear genetic separation from each other.[7] This scientific evidence indicates that our current species are *not* genetically drifting. Ironically, this evidence also confirms the original findings of Georges Cuvier, the renowned founding father of paleontology, who also found that our current species are not evolving.

DNA is like a computer program, but far, far more advanced than any software we've ever created - Bill Gates

Robert Grass, Ph.D. of ETH Zurich, said, "A little after the discovery of the double helix architecture of DNA, people figured out that the coding language of nature is very similar to the binary language we use in computers. On a hard drive, we use 0s and 1s to represent data, and in DNA, we have four nucleotides, A, C, T and G."[24]

DNA is massively superior in storing information than our current computer technology. The sum total of all the world's information, about 2 zettabytes, could not only fit on a four-gram DNA hard drive the size of a teaspoon, but it would also last for thousands of years![25]

Teams of engineers, corporations and governments have made great efforts in advancing our computer technology, and some are now developing DNA-based technology for storage.[25] Did this vastly more advanced DNA technology *really* just *happen* to come into existence?

The entire planet has a near-perfect naturally functioning ecosystem. If someone had designed all of this, it would be universally regarded as an absolutely brilliant masterpiece. And Somebody did. The DNA code of Earth's living creatures could only have been authored by the same unimaginably intelligent Creator.

Scientists have no proof that life was not the result of an act of creation, but they are driven by the nature of their profession to seek explanations for the origin of life that lie within the boundaries of natural law
– Robert Jastrow, of NASA

Earth's Current Creatures Are Not Evolving

A scientific study released in 2018 sheds some light on how long modern humans have existed. The study, "Why should mitochondria define species?" was published in the journal **Human Evolution** by lead author Mark Stoeckle from The Rockefeller University in New York, and David Thaler at the University of Basel in Switzerland.[7]

After examining millions of DNA samples from 100,000 different species from all over the planet, Stoeckle and Thaler concluded that **most of our current animal species emerged nearly simultaneously within the last 200,000 years.** Their conclusions are based on neutral mutation testing, which refers to slight DNA changes that occur across generations. Neutral mutation testing measures DNA "tree rings" or "barcodes" that indicate how many generations old a species is.

They found 90 percent of Earth's existing animals, including humans, all emerged from small populations between 100,000 and 200,000 years ago. They also found **people and animals separated by geographic distance have not become more genetically diverse during the last 200,000 years!** "This conclusion is very surprising, and I fought against it as hard as I could," said Thaler. He was surprised that species have such very clear genetic boundaries, and that it is difficult to find intermediates (missing links). **"If individuals are stars, then species are galaxies.** They are compact clusters in the vastness of empty sequence space." They found, similar to phone numbers, that each species' DNA sequence goes specifically to that species, and none other.

Thaler also commented that the absence of intermediates is something Darwin struggled to understand— "Experts have interpreted low genetic variation among living humans as a result of our recent expansion from a small population in which a sequence from one mother became the ancestor for all modern human mitochondrial sequences."

This ironically supports the findings of Georges Cuvier, the founding father of modern paleontology, who argued in his Great Debate against evolutionary theory in 1830 that our current species are *not* evolving,[55] twenty years before Charles Darwin published *The Origin of Species.*

This also supports the Genesis statement that species were created or made by God to genetically continue "according to their kind," and are not genetically drifting randomly into new species. (Genesis 1:25)

Birds v. Reptiles

Although evolutionary theory logically dictates that flying birds were not the first life forms evolving from ocean creatures, evolutionists are unsure at what point after this that the timing and development of birds took place, in part because scientists haven't found evidence of the wide-spread existence of birds in the Triassic, Jurassic, and Cretaceous Periods.

Some birds are known to exist then, and a few birds may have existed in the Triassic period, but the problem with finding bird fossils is that their tiny bones make their fossils very rare and difficult to find, so this issue may never be adequately resolved.[50]

But, if a dual application is made for the six days of Genesis to also dually describe all six major Eras, then a conflict arises for the fifth Era—Genesis states birds were the significant land creatures during the fifth Mesozoic Era, but scientists have traditionally thought reptilian dinosaurs ruled the Triassic, Jurassic, and Cretaceous Periods (the Mesozoic Era).

Birds being "created" and "blessed" on day five indicates that birds were the significant land creature event of the fifth day (Mesozoic Era), just as humans were the significant land creature event of the sixth day (our current sixth Era). Genesis using "create" indicates the origin and importance of these birds, as opposed to the mammals on day six that were just "made," indicating that mammals played a minor role, and also perhaps that it wasn't their origin but rather that they were modifications from prior mammals of the Mesozoic Era.

This bird conflict does become quite interesting when matching the fifth day of Genesis to the Triassic, Jurassic and Cretaceous Periods of the Mesozoic Era. Some scientists speculate that dinosaurs and birds are closely related.[50,51]

Mary Schweitzer, the respected paleontologist who first discovered soft tissue in a T-rex bone, describes herself as "a complete and total Christian." Dr. Schweitzer said, "If you have all this evidence and proof positive that God exists, you don't need faith. I think He kind of designed it so that we'd never be able to prove His existence. And I think that's really cool." Her astonishing discovery of soft tissue in T-rex bones led to another discovery, that the T-rex may have had red blood cells similar to birds, such as ostriches. Dr. Schweitzer is a fundamental Christian who does not believe in "young earth" creationists' theories.[51]

The Eight Genesis Events of our Era

The Bible and science both state life first began in the ocean (per Job 38:8 the sea burst forth and issued from the womb), then land appears and plants come next, then living creatures, and humans come last.

The eight main Genesis time events in the making and creating of our current sixth Era occurs in a scientific sequence—

> **Light** ⇒ **Atmosphere** ⇒ **Land** ⇒ **Plants** ⇒ **Atmospheric Change** ⇒ **Sea Creatures and Birds** ⇒ **Mammals** ⇒ **Humans**

The first five events prepare for the significant living creatures.[27]

There is only a mere 1 in 40,320 chance of Genesis having these eight events in this order, which modern science just so happens to match.

This powerful evidence gives pause for consideration.

God broadly refers to our entire current sixth Era as being <u>made</u> and not <u>created</u>— "The Lord <u>made</u> the heavens and the earth, the sea, and all that is in them in six days, and rested the seventh day." (Exodus 20:11)

This indicates that God doesn't regard our current Era as being the very first created Era, but as a modification of, or made from, prior Eras. Our Era occurs after the obliteration of most life forms at the end of the Mesozoic Era. In light of this, it is very interesting that the six numerical stages of time events in Genesis explains not only the sequence of events to produce the life forms and animals and humans for our current Era as we now know it, but it also simultaneously gives a broad overview for all six major Eras. So, not only does the six days of Genesis give a broad overview of the exact sequence for how our **current sixth Era** was made, but also at the same time gives the sequence of how all **six major Eras** were made, and does so in the same order and sequence as science says that they occurred! This dual application stems from "yowm" meaning an unspecified length of time, such as an age.

The only possible exception is with God's creation of birds on the fifth day, since many scientists have believed that reptilian dinosaurs were the prominent land-life forms of the fifth Era. But Genesis indicates that birds were the significant land-life forms of the fifth Era.

If you have all this evidence and proof positive that God exists, you don't need faith. I think He kind of designed it so that we'd never be able to prove His existence. And I think that's really cool – Dr. Mary Schweitzer

The Six Major Eras

God's wisdom is often multifaceted, His truth is often multidimensional with many applications. This seems to be true of the six **times** of Genesis, which not only explains both the broad sequence of events for our current sixth Era, but also provides a concise, synoptic description for all six of planet Earth's major Eras—

Era 1 Proterozoic Era/Eon (Age)

God's Spirit hovers over the ocean waters and initializes atmospheric producing life forms, and allows nourishing light to penetrate though the planet's blackening storm soup.

Era 2 Paleozoic Era (Cambrian, Ordovician, Silurian)

Atmospheric producing water-based plant life is made with sea life to maintain and keep them in balance, and an atmosphere is produced under Earth's ultra-dense clouds to prepare for the next Era's life forms.

Era 3 Paleozoic Era (Devonian, Carboniferous)

Dry land appears and advanced land plants are made to thrive in an oxygen rich atmosphere, along with the insects and small creatures needed to maintain and balance these plant populations.

Era 4 The Permian Marine Extinction Gap

The atmosphere clarifies and allows more sunlight and new types of life to be sustained. This important marine and plant life transition prepares an ecosystem and atmosphere to support the creation of large sea and land life on Days 5 and 6. This vital Era is often overlooked.

Era 5 Mesozoic Era (Triassic, Jurassic, and Cretaceous)

The creation and blessing of larger sea creatures and birds (dinosaurs).

Era 6 Cenozoic Era (Tertiary and current Quaternary Period)

The making of our more developed mammals, more reptiles and animals, and finally the creation and blessing of humans.[27]

This ancient Hebrew Genesis text lays out a broad overview of the major ages and creatures in their order of occurrence long before any scientists speculated on how these events took place. Just another 1 in 40,320 coincidence, or more powerful evidence?

Genesis 1 is a dual simultaneous elucidation for explaining both—

1) The six-stage development of our current Cenozoic Era.
2) The six stages and generations for all six major Eras.

www.ingramcontent.com/pod-product-compliance
Lightning Source LLC
Chambersburg PA
CBHW071229090426
42736CB00014B/3022